HOME MADE CHRISTMAS

FOR SOPHIE

EDITOR Holly Dolce
DESIGNER Liam Flanagan
PRODUCTION MANAGER Kathleen Gaffney

Library of Congress Control Number: 2017956827

ISBN: 978-1-4197-3238-6
eISBN: 978-1-68335-323-2

Printed and bound in China
10 9 8 7 6 5 4 3 2 1

Abrams books are available at special discounts when purchased in
quantity for premiums and promotions as well as fundraising or
educational use. Special editions can also be created to specification.
For details, contact specialsales@abramsbooks.com or the address below.

Abrams® is a registered trademark of Harry N. Abrams, Inc.

ABRAMS The Art of Books
195 Broadway, New York, NY 10007
abramsbooks.com

HOME MADE CHRISTMAS

YVETTE VAN BOVEN
PHOTOGRAPHY BY OOF VERSCHUREN

ABRAMS, NEW YORK

CONTENTS

PREFACE

Indeed, reader, here it is: a comprehensive Christmas cookbook by Van Boven! Most of the questions you sent me are about hosting dinner parties. How to plan them. What to cook when you're having more than four guests. How much can be prepared in advance in order to avoid losing control during the evening. How to prevent a total panic attack.

Throughout the years, I've written tons of winter holiday recipes and stress-prevention tips for all sorts of magazines and newspapers. Therefore I figured it would be a good idea to bundle them together into a book, providing you with an easy-to-use overview.

It was when composing *Home Sweet Home*, my book on Irish comfort food, that I discovered just how many holiday recipes I had written. The Irish and I are avid celebrators, after all, of Christmas and other occasions. And just like that, my chapter on Christmas grew into a whole separate book.

In this Christmas book I will guide you through the winter holidays. I will give you tips on how to prevent things from getting out of hand and how to avoid panicking. I will give you easy, foolproof recipes that can be prepared ahead of time so that you too can be merry while hosting your dinner. Whenever possible the recipe directions are divided into pre-preparation and preparation parts, so you know in advance what you're up against. Often all that is needed before serving is some reheating or the sophisticated placement of a sprig of parsley. You can do this. I will even throw in a stack of menus so you don't have to worry about those, either.

Perhaps you will be celebrating your first romantic Christmas with the love of your life. Maybe you are hosting your in-laws, with all your cousins, nephews, and nieces in tow. Whatever your situation, we will come up with a workable plan, making sure you have everything you need to pull this off.

And . . . if you don't celebrate Christmas but simply feel like having a cozy winter dinner, this book will come in very handy as well.

Be merry,

x YVETTE

A Few Words on the Ingredients

Number of people

Each recipe serves four, unless otherwise noted. Christmas dinner parties tend to be large, so you will also find recipes that serve many more. When cooking for fewer guests, you can halve the amounts . . . or eat your meal two days in a row. Simple as that.

Measurements

1 tablespoon = 15 ml
1 coffee spoon = 7 ml
1 teaspoon = 5 ml

Oven

Each oven has its own baking characteristics. Some get hotter, others are slower. It could be that your oven takes longer or shorter than the baking times I use in the recipes. These baking times are therefore guidelines. So by all means, rely on your own experience with your own oven and always use an oven thermometer.

Broth

Home made broth is always the best choice, so I won't be repeating this in every recipe. Any dish, no matter how simple, will greatly benefit from the rich and intense flavor of a home-brewed broth. Bouillon cubes or canned or boxed broth make for an easy substitute—of course I understand that not everyone has the time to make their own broth—but they aren't the most flavorful solution. Therefore I use cubes sparingly and always make sure to freeze my home made broth in small portions. Besides, you can't beat the smell of a pot of broth gently simmering on the stove. It's the easiest way to make use of that chicken carcass, along with leftover celeriac, carrots, and leeks from the fridge.

You can find several broth recipes in the "Basics" section (page 254).

Eggs

I prefer to use large eggs. Organic farm eggs can vary widely in size. If you are afraid your eggs are too small, simply use two instead of one. Not having enough egg in a recipe can really make a difference.

Milk

I prefer to use whole milk. The high fat percentage is where the flavor is.

Olive oil

I use flavorful, good-quality olive oil, usually extra virgin, for finishing. I also use it for cooking, because I can taste it in the final dish. I've stopped specifying it in my ingredient lists. Unless stated otherwise, "olive oil" means intense, extra-virgin oil of prime quality.

Meat

I used to be much stricter and consistently added "organic" to the meats in my ingredient lists. Today I feel that people should make their own decisions about the meat they buy. Anyway, not everyone shares my ideals and—yes, I know—organic meat is way more expensive. I go by the maxim: Eat less meat, and if you do eat it, buy organic meat from animals that had a decent life. That's how I do it. Better for the animals and for our planet. In this book I will give you many vegetarian recipes or suggestions for where you can omit the meat.

READ ON WHY DON'T YOU?

CHRISTMAS STRESS-RELIEF TIPS

Lists

Make lists, at least two to three days in advance, preferably even earlier. Not only for the groceries but also for the menu. What will you prepare beforehand and what will you finish on the evening itself? This will prevent that moment of realization the minute your guests have finished their plates: Oh! I forgot to add the . . . !

Ordering special ingredients

Order any special ingredients well in advance, and buy as many groceries in advance as possible. This way you don't risk having to run out and buy essential items on the day of the big dinner. Often the stores will be sold out of popular holiday foods, which won't make cooking any easier or more enjoyable. Most grocery stores, delicatessens, fishmongers, and butchers will allow you to place orders with no problem.

Don't make things more complicated

Choose dishes that are easy to prepare ahead of time and only require some finishing touches on the evening itself. Like they do in a professional restaurant! This prevents cooking stress and allows you to join your guests with a glass of wine.

Pans

If you haven't cooked grand dinners before but intend to do so now, it's a good idea to determine which pans you'll need for each dish. Then try to limit the number of pans you use so you won't run out of pans or stovetop or oven space.

DON'T FORGET TO BUY EXTRA TRASH BAGS

AND CANDLES

Clean up

Clean out the fridge and the freezer a week before the holidays. You will need the storage space—much more of it than usual. The drinks especially will take up a lot of fridge space.

Vegetarians

When you have one or more vegetarian dinner guests, you don't have to make dishes especially for them; instead pick a recipe that allows you to prepare the meat or fish separately. Leave out the chicken from the soup and serve it alongside, or replace the salmon in a salad with some crumbled goat cheese. Or simply opt for a completely vegetarian menu. This way you'll only have to cook once while also being oh so modern, because not eating any meat or fish is very *au courant*.

Hospitality = calmness

Make sure your guests receive something to drink right away, and place some snacks on the table. Some delicious bread and butter, thinly sliced cured ham, smoked almonds—anything tasty, really: You have plenty of choice in this department. This will buy you some extra time before dinner has to be served. Don't overdo it, though, or your guests will have lost their appetite by the time you have prepared the appetizers.

Think!

Don't let your menu consist of exclusively oven dishes: Naturally they won't all simultaneously fit in your oven! Chose a premade dessert, for instance, and a soup that is ready and sits in a pan on the stove waiting to be served while the main dish is roasting in the oven. This is how you create a menu that is easier to execute.

Would you rather not think about menu planning at all? I included several menus at the end of this book, purely for your convenience, starting on page 272.

Ready-made

Don't make things too complicated for yourself. Select doable recipes, dishes that you may have cooked before. Otherwise try to buy certain items on your menu premade. Some cream puffs (page 246), or cheeses and charcuterie. This will save you a lot of time and energy so that you can put all your effort into your very own *pièce de résistance*.

Forgot to chill your bubbles?

No worries: Tightly wrap the bottles in a damp dish-cloth and put them in the freezer. Since the wet cloth will conduct the temperature faster than air, your bottle of champagne will be ice cold in less than twenty minutes. You can also place the bottle in a wine cooler filled with ice cubes and water to which you added a scoop of salt. Your bubbles will be nicely chilled in no time.

ANYTHING YOU CAN PREPARE BEFOREHAND CAN BE STORED IN THE FREEZER (SOUPS, CAKE LAYERS, ETC.)!

DON'T FORGET TO TAKE IT OUT IN ADVANCE...

Wine selection

If you don't know anything about wine, go to your wine store and tell them about your menu. Also explain how much you'd like to spend per bottle. Your wine specialist will be able offer you the advice you need.

HAVE ALL DRINKS DELIVERED TO YOUR HOME, YOU'RE CARRYING ENOUGH AS IT IS...

Warm plates

I *really* believe that warm plates are essential. Often, by the time that everyone is seated, the wine is poured, and dinner is being served, the food will be nearly cold. Heat the plates by placing them in the oven at a medium temperature. If your oven happens to be packed with food already, you can quickly put the plates through the dishwasher, running a short cycle. You can also place them in a tub of hot water or wrap them in a damp dish towel and heat them up in the microwave.

How much wine?

A bottle serves six people, one glass each. For a Christmas dinner, it's safe to count on at least one bottle per guest. There will always be people who drink less and those who drink more, but this way you will be safe. If in doubt you can ask your wine seller.

Enough silverware?

After you have decided upon your menu, make an inventory of your silverware: Do you have enough for your big party? It's nice to know beforehand instead of finding it out on the night of your dinner. Perhaps your neighbors or family can help you out if you're short.

SET THE TABLE A DAY IN ADVANCE. SOUNDS EXTREME, BUT IT WILL SAVE YOU A LOT OF STRESS.

Accept help

Make use of the expertise of the people in the stores where you get your groceries. The butcher knows best which cut to use for a certain dish. The fishmonger will gladly clean or fillet your red snapper, and the produce manager will no doubt be able to order those heirloom greens you need. Often he will be able to source vegetables he doesn't normally carry in his store if you ask him to. This will make your life easier.

Setting a mood

Keep in mind that warm Christmas dinner memories aren't all about the food but just as much about the atmosphere.

Less = more

Don't forget! A joyful atmosphere matters more than a tableful of artfully crafted dishes.

Be merry

Set the table to bring about the right mood and make sure you are in a cheerful mood as well. Believe me, this is half the trick. Even if something didn't turn out quite the way you wanted, being a merry host remains key. Because that is what your guests will remember in the end. Well, honestly, they'll also remember your miserably failed risotto, but you'll be laughing about that in due time.

Be realistic

Peeling vegetables is time consuming. Allow room for that in your planning. Start well in advance or ask for assistance: Kids are great at these kinds of tasks. This is how my sister and I learned to cook.

HANDY TO-DO LIST
FOR AN ENORMOUS DINNER PARTY

1 MONTH IN ADVANCE

SEND OUT INVITATIONS SO YOU KNOW HOW MANY GUESTS TO EXPECT.

WILL YOU COME TO MY DINNER PARTY?

2 WEEKS IN ADVANCE

DECIDE ON THE MENU AND THEREFORE ON THE WINE. ORDER THE WINE & ANY HARD-TO-FIND INGREDIENTS. (ONLINE!)

1 WEEK IN ADVANCE

CLEAN OUT FRIDGE & FREEZER. START PREPARING THINGS (SOUP, CAKE BOTTOMS THAT CAN BE STORED IN THE FREEZER).

SEVERAL DAYS IN ADVANCE

CHECK YOUR SILVERWARE:
DO YOU HAVE ENOUGH?
IF NOT: ASK YOUR NEIGHBORS TO LEND YOU SOME.
COUNT YOUR PANS, OVEN DISHES.
DO YOU HAVE ENOUGH CHAIRS?
IF NOT, CALL THE NEIGHBORS.
POLISH THE SILVERWARE.
IRON NAPKINS AND THE TABLECLOTH.
ENOUGH GLASSES?
WATER PITCHERS?
SERVING SPOONS?
TEA LIGHTS OR CANDLES?

AT LEAST THE SILVERWARE IS GETTING SOME SHINE.

2 DAYS IN ADVANCE

→ GET ALL YOUR GROCERIES. ←

DECIDE ON WHAT TO WEAR
(THERE'S STILL TIME TO WASH IT.)

...AND TO IRON IT!

ON THE DAY ITSELF

MAKE SURE THE DOG HAS
BEEN WALKED EXTENSIVELY.

AND ALONG THE WAY PICK
SOME IVY FOR YOUR TABLE.
CONTINUE COOKING.
FOR EACH COURSE, PUT
EVERYTHING THAT SHOULD
BE ADDED AT THE LAST
MINUTE IN PLACE.
HANG THE ENTIRE MENU
IN A VISIBLE SPOT IN YOUR
KITCHEN SO YOU WON'T
FORGET ANYTHING.

SET OUT EVERYTHING YOU NEED
FOR THE DRINKS. (IF GUESTS SHOW
UP EARLY — TOO EARLY! — YOU'LL BE PREPARED.)

1 DAY IN ADVANCE

MAKE EVERYTHING THAT
CAN BE PREPARED NOW.
DON'T FORGET THINGS
LIKE DRESSINGS.
CHILL THE DRINKS.
SET THE TABLE.
TIDY THE HOUSE.

CHOP

LIGHT THE CANDLES AND START
UP THE FIREPLACE...
TIDY UP THE LAST MESS IN
THE KITCHEN. MAKE
SURE THE DISHWASHER IS EMPTY.

QUICKLY JUMP IN THE SHOWER.
PUT ON YOUR PARTY OUTFIT
& COMB YOUR HAIR.

DING DONG!

THE DAY AFTER

SLEEP IN — MAKE COFFEE.
READ THE PAPER.
CLEAN UP & BRING YOUR
NEIGHBORS A NICE
BOTTLE FOR LETTING
YOU BORROW
THEIR STUFF.

THANKS GUYS!

THE MORNING

BRIOCHE & RED FRUIT SWIRLS WITH RICOTTA GLAZE

Makes 10 substantial rolls

FOR THE BRIOCHE SWIRLS

¼ cup (60 ml) lukewarm milk

⅓ cup (60 g) granulated sugar

2¼ teaspoons (1 envelope) active dry yeast

2¾ cups (350 g) all-purpose flour, plus plenty for dusting

¼ teaspoon salt

3 eggs, beaten

9 tablespoons (125 g) butter, at room temperature, cubed

½ cup (100 g) light brown sugar

10½ ounces (300 g) frozen red fruit, preferably a mix

FOR THE RICOTTA GLAZE

3 to 4 tablespoons ricotta

About 2 cups (200 g) sifted confectioners' sugar

Prepare

In a bowl, beat the milk together with the granulated sugar and yeast and let stand for 7 minutes, until the mixture starts foaming. Combine the flour and salt in a large bowl. Form an indentation in the middle. Pour in the yeast mixture and the beaten eggs, then gently combine into a smooth dough. Remove from the bowl and knead for 5 minutes on a floured countertop until supple and soft. Add two cubes of butter and continue kneading until they are incorporated into the dough. Repeat until all the butter has been used and the dough has become shiny and elastic, dusting the countertop with flour as you work and using a bench knife or spatula to scrape up the dough as needed—it may take a while to incorporate all that butter, but be persistent. Place the ball in a greased bowl, cover with plastic wrap, and allow to rise for 90 minutes.

Again briefly knead the dough. Roll out on a lightly floured countertop into a 16 by 24-inch (40 by 60-cm) rectangle. Sprinkle with the brown sugar and frozen fruit. Now, roll up from a short side into a short, thick log. Wrap in plastic wrap. Place the roll in the freezer for 15 minutes to firm up, which will make slicing it easier later on.

Remove the plastic wrap. Using a sharp knife, cut the log into ten even slices. Place them on parchment paper–lined baking sheets, a little apart (they are still rising!). Cover loosely with plastic wrap and allow to continue rising for 30 minutes in a warm, draft-free spot. If you'd like to make these the evening before, let them rise overnight in the fridge on the baking sheets.

Make

Allow brioches that were stored in the fridge 30 to 45 minutes to reach room temperature before you proceed.

Meanwhile, preheat the oven to 350°F (180°C).

Uncover the brioches and bake for 30 to 35 minutes, until golden brown. Let cool for a few minutes.

For the glaze, whisk the ricotta in a bowl and add confectioners' sugar until you get a thick glaze with the consistency of whole milk yogurt. Drizzle over the buns. Let stand briefly to set the glaze, then serve warm or at room temperature.

WENTELTEEFJES, OR SAVORY FRENCH TOAST (THE DUTCH VERSION)

*Makes 6 to 8 slices,
depending on size of bread*

4 large eggs

½ cup (125 ml) milk

½ cup (125 ml) heavy cream

1 teaspoon mustard

½ cup (50 g) grated Parmesan
cheese, plus extra for serving

A pinch of sea salt

Freshly ground black pepper

A few drops of Tabasco sauce

1 tablespoon Worcestershire sauce

6 to 8 slices of good-quality white
bread; you can make lovely
shapes using a cutter

Some butter for frying

FOR GARNISH

A salad of chopped fresh garden
herbs such as chives, flat-leaf
parsley, and/or basil and some
arugula with a simple olive oil
and vinegar vinaigrette

Wentelteefjes can be sweet, but they are tasty savory as well. Perfect for using up old bread, they make for an addictive Christmas breakfast.

Prepare

Whisk the eggs, milk, cream, and mustard until foamy. Stir in the cheese, season with some salt and pepper, a little Tabasco, and a splash of Worcestershire sauce. Pour the egg mixture into a shallow bowl. You can prepare the egg mixture the night before and store it in the fridge overnight.

Make

Place two slices of bread in the bowl—or as many you can fit, really—and let them soak for 1 to 2 minutes.

Over medium heat, melt a cube of butter in a nonstick skillet and cook the soaked bread for about 2 minutes per side, until golden brown. Let drain on some paper towels while frying the remaining slices.

Sprinkle with cheese and serve with the green herb salad.

CHRISTMAS WREATH BREAD

Serves about 8

FOR THE DOUGH

1 cup (250 ml) milk

3½ tablespoons (50 g) butter, cubed

2¼ teaspoons (1 envelope) active dry yeast

3½ cups (450 g) all-purpose flour

¼ cup (50 g) lightly packed light brown sugar

½ teaspoon sea salt

FOR THE FILLING

1⅓ cups (200 g) currants

⅓ cup (50 g) chopped succade (preserved or crystallized fruit)

1 teaspoon ground cinnamon

1 teaspoon mixed spice (*speculaaskruiden*)

Zest and juice of 1 lemon

Zest and juice of 1 orange

7 tablespoons (100 g) butter, at room temperature

2 tablespoons light brown sugar

1 egg, lightly beaten

Confectioners' sugar for serving (optional)

First make the dough. In a saucepan, heat the milk until just below boiling, then add the butter and remove from the heat. Allow to cool for 5 minutes—until just below body temperature—then add the yeast to the now lukewarm milk. Let stand for another 10 minutes.

Combine the flour, brown sugar, and salt in a large bowl and form an indentation in the center. Pour in the milk mixture. Using a wooden spoon, combine until the dough holds together. Continue kneading with your hands on a lightly floured countertop for another 10 minutes.

Shape into a ball, place in a greased bowl, cover, and let rise in a warm spot for 90 minutes, or until it has doubled in volume.

For the filling, heat the currants, succade, cinnamon, mixed spice, and the lemon and orange zest and juice in a saucepan. Cook over very low heat, until the currants are nicely plumped up. Let cool. Mix in the butter and brown sugar and set aside.

Knead the dough briefly once more. On a lightly floured countertop, roll it out into a rectangle about 18 by 12 inches (45 by 30 cm). Spread the filling over it using a pancake spatula. Allow a margin of about ¾ inch (2 cm) at the long sides.

Roll up the dough from a long side, moisten the bare edge with water, and press to seal the seam. Place the roll with the seam facing down. Moisten the ends of the roll as well and bend them together, forming a circle. Place the wreath on a baking sheet lined with parchment paper.

With a sharp knife, cut into the roll every 1¼ inches (3 cm), almost all the way through, but not quite. Pull out each cut piece, exposing the sides, and the spirals will form a circular fan of swirls. Cover with a clean dish towel and allow the wreath to rise again for about 45 minutes.

Preheat the oven to 400°F (200°C).

Brush the bread with the lightly beaten egg. Bake for about 30 minutes, until golden brown. Optionally, dust with confectioners' sugar.

CLASSIC MINI MINCE PIES

Makes about 24 tartlets

FOR THE DOUGH

2 cups (250 g) all-purpose flour

2 tablespoons superfine sugar

9 tablespoons (125 g) chilled butter, cubed

1 egg yolk

A pinch of salt

Juice of 1 orange

FOR THE FILLING

About 1 cup plus 2 tablespoons (350 g) mincemeat (page 261)

Superfine or confectioners' sugar, for serving

ALSO NEEDED

Mini muffin pan

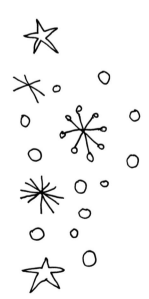

Of course they have to come out of a mini muffin pan: small two-bite pies, mincemeat-filled orange-flavored crusts with a star shape on top. Although a heart or some other Christmas shape is fine too!

It works best if you pulse the dough in a food processor to ensure the butter stays cold.

Combine the flour, superfine sugar, butter, egg yolk, and salt until the mixture resembles coarse crumbs. Add the orange juice drop by drop until the dough is holding together. Shape into a flattened ball, wrap with plastic wrap, and set aside in the fridge for a couple of hours.

Preheat the oven to 400°F (200°C). Thoroughly grease the cups of the mini muffin pan with butter or baking spray.

On a floured countertop, roll out the dough into a slab ¼ inch (½ cm) thick. Use a cookie cutter or a glass to cut out rounds about ⅜ inch (1 cm) larger than the diameter of the cups. Gently press them into the cups. If the dough tears, don't worry; just press lightly to fix it. Fill the tartlets with a generous coffee spoon or small tablespoon of mincemeat each.

Gather all the leftover pieces of dough and roll them out into a thin slab again. Cut stars (or other shapes) using a cookie cutter. Place the shapes on top of the filling and lightly press.

Bake the tartlets for 10 to 15 minutes. They should lightly brown, although not too dark! Let cool in the pan for 3 minutes before scooping them out with a knife so they can cool further. Now you can use your muffin pan for another round if necessary.

Once cool, dust them with superfine or confectioners' sugar.

KRISPY CHRISTMAS WREATHS

Makes about 10 cookies

8½ tablespoons (120 g) butter

¼ cup (60 ml) syrup, preferably golden syrup

¼ cup (25 g) cocoa powder

¼ cup (30 g) confectioners' sugar

¼ cup (35 g) dried cranberries (or other dried fruit)

3 to 4 handfuls of cornflakes or crispy rice cereal

15 to 20 Bigarreaux cherries, halved

Melt the butter and syrup in a saucepan, stir in the cocoa powder, and remove from the heat. Fold in the confectioners' sugar, cranberries, and cornflakes. Carefully combine until everything is coated with the butter mixture, but not wet. If necessary, add more cornflakes.

Line a baking sheet that's small enough to fit in your fridge with parchment paper.

Use two spoons to form little heaps of the cornflakes mixture on the baking sheet. Using the back of a spoon, form holes in the middle of each, creating little wreaths. Decorate with the halved cherries.

Put the cookies in the fridge for 3 to 4 hours to firm up completely before you dig in.

SQUASH, FETA & SAGE PULL-APART BREAD

Serves about 6, depending on what else is offered at the table

1 cup (250 ml) lukewarm water

2 teaspoons honey (or sugar)

2¼ teaspoons (1 envelope) instant yeast

3 cups plus 2 tablespoons (400 g) all-purpose flour

1 teaspoon sea salt, plus a little extra

About 14 ounces (400 g) butternut squash (about ½ squash), peeled and cubed

A splash of olive oil for greasing

Freshly ground black pepper

1 teaspoon paprika

3½ ounces (100 g) feta cheese, cut into ⅜-inch (1-cm) cubes

12 fresh sage leaves, 4 leaves finely chopped

1 egg, beaten

In a pitcher, combine the lukewarm water with the honey and yeast. Let stand for 7 minutes, or until it begins to foam and all the yeast has dissolved.

Mix the flour and 1 teaspoon salt in a wide bowl and form an indentation in the middle. Pour the yeast mixture into the indentation. Stir until the dough starts to hold together and continue kneading for at least 10 minutes on a floured countertop until you have a soft and supple dough that is no longer sticky and bounces back when you poke it. Place the ball in a greased bowl, cover with plastic wrap, and set aside for 1 hour in a warm and draft-free spot so the dough can rise and double in size.

Preheat the oven to 400°F (200°C).

Spread the squash cubes out on a greased baking sheet, sprinkle with salt, pepper, and paprika, and roast for 30 minutes, or until they are just tender and the edges begin to brown. Let cool.

After the dough has risen, knead it again briefly. Grease a rectangular 9 by 5-inch (23 by 12-cm) loaf pan with oil.

Roll the dough out into a 6 by 10-inch (15 by 25-cm) rectangle. Sprinkle with the squash cubes, feta, and chopped sage, leaving the edges clear. Roll up the dough from a short side into a thick log. Cut the log into twelve equal slices and quickly roll those into balls. Arrange six of them in the bottom of the loaf pan and place a sage leaf on each ball. Then place more dough balls on top of each, seams alternating, until the pan is filled. Stick the rest of the sage leaves in between the balls. Cover with a clean cloth and let rise again, this time for only 30 minutes.

Preheat the oven to 400°F (200°C) again. Brush the dough with the egg and bake for about 30 minutes, until golden brown. Allow to cool on a rack for 5 minutes, remove from the pan, and allow to cool completely.

Serve with soup or a big salad.

APPLE-CRANBERRY CHRISTMAS ROLLS

Makes 6 substantial rolls

6 tablespoons plus 1 teaspoon
(90 g) butter

½ cup plus 2 tablespoons (125 g)
sugar, plus a little extra

2 eggs

½ cup (125 g) applesauce,
home made or from a jar

About ⅓ cup (70 ml) milk

3 cups plus 2 tablespoons (400 g)
all-purpose flour, sifted

A pinch of salt

Zest of ½ lemon

⅔ cup (100 g) dried cranberries

1 apple, peeled and diced

Confectioners' sugar

Prepare

Beat the butter together with the sugar for about 3 minutes, until smooth and creamy. Add the eggs, one at the time. While beating, add the applesauce and milk, then spoon in the sifted flour, then the salt, lemon zest, cranberries, and apple. The dough should be nice and soft, not too dry. If needed, add a few drops of milk. Grease six muffin tins. Fill them with the apple-cranberry mixture. (Or do as I do: Use a large ice cream scoop to form six to eight balls of batter and place them on a parchment paper–lined baking sheet.)

Let stand for 15 minutes before baking. You can also prepare them the evening before and store them in a cool place.

Make

Preheat the oven to 335°F (170°C).

Bake the rolls for 40 to 45 minutes. Dust with confectioners' sugar. They are best when still a bit warm.

SAUSAGE BUNS WITH FENNEL

Makes about 10 buns

A knob of butter

1 red onion, finely diced

1 smallish fennel bulb, cored and diced

3 to 4 tablespoons red wine, vermouth, or water

18 ounces (500 g) fresh pork sausages, preferably with fennel seeds

About ¾ cup (70 g) fresh breadcrumbs (made from day-old bread; otherwise use store-bought)

1 teaspoon fennel seeds, crushed in a mortar, plus a little extra for sprinkling

½ teaspoon caraway seeds, crushed in a mortar

Sea salt and freshly ground black pepper

1 (17.3-ounce/490-g) box frozen puff pastry dough (2 sheets), thawed

1 egg, beaten

LITTLE SIDE NOTE

As long as I can remember, we have been calling these *worstenbroodjes*, or sausage buns, at our house. Since they are made with puff pastry they should technically be called *saucijzenbroodjes*, or sausage turnovers. But my parents proudly hail from the southern Dutch province of Limburg, an area where the word *worstenbroodje* is so deeply rooted that I have simply always associated it with Christmas food. When hearing "sausage *turnover*," on the other hand, I think more of a greasy pastry you pick up at a train station.

In my book *Home Made Winter*, I told you the story of how my mother, Mariëtte, would bake a whole batch of sausage buns at the beginning of each winter break. We would eat them throughout the holidays: for breakfast, as a snack, for lunch, a lazy dinner, or while lounging on the sofa, watching a Christmas movie on TV. Now, several years later, her recipe has traveled the globe, and people from all over have been sending me pictures of their own Christmas buns. I love it!

Now I'd like to add a new recipe to your repertoire. These sausage buns are really delicious as well—and easy to make, to boot—as long as you buy the right type of sausage. (I love a fennel seed, red wine sausage made by Dutch artisans Brandt & Levie, but you can find your own freshly made local variety.) Basically all you have to do is swaddle it in a blanket of dough.

In a large frying pan, melt the butter over medium heat. Add the onion and fennel and fry, stirring now and then. After 5 minutes, pour in several tablespoons of the wine and continue cooking until tender, about 15 minutes, adding more liquid if needed to keep the vegetables from sticking. Remove from the heat and let cool somewhat on the counter.

Preheat the oven to 400°F (200°C).

Remove the casings from the sausages and crumble the meat in a mixing bowl. Combine the fried onion and fennel with the meat, add the breadcrumbs, fennel seeds, and caraway seeds. Knead together until homogenous. Season to taste with a couple pinches of salt and pepper if necessary, but be careful: The sausages themselves are already seasoned!

Line a rimmed baking sheet with parchment paper.

Divide the sausage mixture into ten balls. Using your wet hands, shape them into sausage-sized logs (about 4½ inches/11 cm long). Set aside.

Roll out each sheet of puff pastry to an 11-inch (28-cm) square. Cut each into six rectangles (cut in half one way, then into thirds the other way). You'll need ten rectangles total; set two rectangles aside for another use.

Place each sausage log in the center of a puff pastry rectangle, brush one long side of each dough rectangle with a bit of the beaten egg, and wrap the dough around the sausage, pinching the seam and ends together very securely—if these leak as they bake, the bottoms will get soggy, so take care to seal them well. Place on the prepared baking sheet, seams down. Brush the tops with more beaten egg and sprinkle with some fennel seeds. Bake for about 25 minutes, until nicely golden brown.

Once cooled and wrapped, you can store them in the fridge for the rest of your Christmas break (about a week), so why not make a whole lot of them?

OATMEAL PANCAKES

Makes about 16 pancakes

2¼ cups (200 g) rolled oats

2 teaspoons baking powder

½ teaspoon plus a pinch of salt

1 teaspoon cinnamon

4 eggs, separated

¾ cup plus 1 tablespoon (200 ml) milk

A little butter for cooking

FOR ON TOP

Cranberry compote (see page 266)

Some fruit, melted butter, golden syrup, maple syrup, or confectioners' sugar

This is a recipe for the fluffiest, most delicious pancakes ever. I know I've said this before in my book *Home Made Summer*, but it's true. I did manage to improve my own recipe. Man, oh man, how wonderful these are. And to complete a truly royal Christmas breakfast you can serve them along with my cranberry compote.

Grind the oatmeal into fine flour in a food processor. This will take just a sec.

Add the baking powder, ½ teaspoon salt, and the cinnamon and combine by pressing the pulse button a few times. In a bowl, whisk the egg yolks together with the milk and add the dry ingredients from the processor, stirring to combine.

In a clean bowl, with a clean whisk, whisk the egg whites and a pinch of salt until stiff. Fold into the batter.

Heat a small lump of butter in a nonstick skillet. Spoon in a ladle of batter and cook three pancakes at a time over low to medium heat. Use a pancake spatula to flip them when the underside has browned and cook for another 2 minutes.

Serve with some delicious toppings, and dust with confectioners' sugar if you like.

CRUNCHY BLACKBERRY & APPLE COCOTTES

Makes 2 large or 4 small cocottes, or 1 large oven dish

1¾ cups (250 g) blackberries

1 apple, peeled and diced

Heaping ¼ cup (60 g) packed dark brown sugar

1 teaspoon cinnamon

A pinch of salt

2½ cups (250 g) granola

4 tablespoons (55 g) butter, at room temperature, plus more for the baking dishes

Prepare

Grease the cocottes or baking dishes with some butter.

Combine the blackberries and apple with the brown sugar, cinnamon, and salt.

In another bowl, mix the granola with the butter.

Divide the blackberry-apple mixture among the cocottes and, if you want to bake them right away, sprinkle with the granola mixture. If you are preparing for the next day, keep the granola mixture separate, cover everything, and store the fruit-filled cocottes in the fridge until you are ready to bake.

Make

Preheat the oven to 350°F (180°C).

Spoon the granola mixture on top of the fruit in the cocottes. Bake for about 25 minutes, until the fruit is bubbling and the granola is nicely crunchy. Serve with some yogurt or crème anglaise (page 255).

SCOTTISH EGGS

*Serves 4 as a brunch
or lunch dish*

6 eggs, as fresh as possible

2 small handfuls of all-purpose
flour

About 3⅓ cups (100 g) cornflakes,
finely ground

1 pound 5 ounces (600 g) nice
sausages (I prefer chunky, fresh
ones from an artisanal producer)

Vegetable oil for deep-frying

Sea salt and freshly ground black
pepper

Mustard for serving

Prepare

Place 4 eggs in a saucepan, add water until they're well submerged. Bring to a boil, cover, and let stand for 4 minutes. Rinse the eggs with ice-cold water or place them in ice water. Carefully peel them.

Put the flour in one bowl. Whisk the 2 remaining eggs in a second bowl. Put the ground cornflakes in a third bowl.

Remove the casings from the sausages. Divide the meat into four portions. In the palm of your hand, press the meat into a thin patty. Carefully wrap it around one of the soft-boiled eggs. Secure it by gently pressing while making sure not to damage the egg. Now roll the wrapped egg in the flour. Gently tap to remove any excess. Dip it in the beaten eggs, then roll it in the cornflakes. Repeat for the rest of the eggs and sausage.

Allow the balls to firm up in the fridge for 1 hour. Longer is also fine, of course, up to overnight.

Make

Heat 2 inches (5 cm) of the oil in a wok or deep-fryer. If you have a thermometer, the oil should reach a temperature of about 335°F (170°C)—not too hot. Deep-fry the balls until nicely golden brown and crispy, 5 to 6 minutes, turning them over halfway through.

Serve the Scottish eggs while still warm, with some mustard on the side.

GINGER HOT CHOCOLATE WITH ROASTED MARSHMALLOWS

Makes 3 to 4 mugs

2¼ cups (500 ml) milk

2 tablespoons peeled and finely grated fresh ginger

3½ ounces (100 g) good-quality dark chocolate (at least 70% cacao), in chunks

2 to 3 handfuls of marshmallows

A pinch of ground ginger

Heat the milk with the ginger, but don't let it boil. Let simmer over very low heat for 10 minutes. Remove from the heat and add the chocolate but don't stir yet. Cover and let stand for 5 minutes. Using a small whisk, stir the chocolate with the milk until thoroughly combined, then pour the mixture through a sieve to remove the solids.

Using a metal skewer, roast the marshmallows over a gas burner, with a brûlée torch (that's what I do), over a candle, or in the fireplace.

Fill three or four mugs three-quarters full with the hot chocolate and divide the marshmallows among them. Sprinkle with ground ginger and serve immediately.

CHAMPAGNE BOWL

WITH CRANBERRY, POMEGRANATE & CLEMENTINE

Makes 20 glasses

2¼ cups (500 ml) sweetened cranberry juice

2¼ cups (500 ml) pomegranate juice

3¼ cups (750 ml) freshly squeezed clementine juice (from about 7 clementines)

5 slices fresh ginger

3 bay leaves

1 bunch fresh mint, leaves only

A handful of fresh cranberries for garnish

Generous amount of ice cubes

2 (750-ml) bottles sparkling wine or champagne

Mix the juices in a large bowl. Add the ginger, bay leaves, and half of the mint and let steep overnight or at least 4 hours.

Place the bowl on the serving table. Decorate with the rest of the fresh mint leaves and the cranberries. Fill large glasses half full with ice cubes, fill halfway with the juice, and top up with champagne. Serve with stirrers.

CRANBERRY MARGARITAS

Serves 4

2 handfuls of ice cubes

¾ cup plus 1 tablespoon (200 ml)
    pure cranberry juice

7 tablespoons (100 ml) freshly
    squeezed lime juice (from 2 to
    3 limes)

½ cup plus 2 tablespoons (150 ml)
    tequila

7 tablespoons (100 ml) orange-
    flavored liqueur, like Cointreau or
    triple sec

FOR GARNISH

1 lime, quartered

Coarse salt on a plate

This recipe yields four glasses in one fell swoop. While it may be fun to prepare individual cocktails for your guests, it can take a while if you have to do it one glass at a time. Check your pantry to see if you have a large canning jar. It can do double duty as a shaker, and you'll be done faster. Merry, merry cranberry!

Chill the glasses by putting an ice cube in each and swirling it around.

Put the remaining ice, the cranberry juice, lime juice, tequila, and orange liqueur in a large (at least 1-quart/1-liter) canning jar with a rubber ring in the lid and seal it tightly. Shake the jar thoroughly, for at least 30 seconds, so the cocktail is nice and cold.

Throw out the ice cubes in the glasses. Rub a lime quarter around the rim of each glass and press the rim in the plate with salt, so that you end up with a salt rim.

Pour the drink from the canning jar into the glasses through a little sieve, or if that's difficult: pour it first through a sieve into another jar and then into the glasses. Serve immediately, of course.

SLOE GIN

Makes about 6½ cups (1.5 liters)

About 18 ounces (500 g) sloe berries (don't measure too precisely)

4½ cups (1 liter) gin

About ½ cup (100 g) sugar, or more to taste

Sloe gin (or actually sloe berry gin) is a staple of an Irish or English Christmas. This is actually hardly a recipe. If you pick them in October and put them in the gin, you can drink sloe gin at Christmas, but it's even better to wait a year or two. The flavor will only improve, and since the berries are soaked in alcohol they'll keep almost indefinitely.

As soon as the berries of the sloe bush are soft enough that they burst open when you squeeze them, they are ripe for picking. Wear gloves! It's a *thorny* bush, and you can injure yourself severely if you forget gloves.

Can't find berries to pick? Use a forager app on your smart phone—a brilliant invention. I am lucky: My aunt Emilie has a sloe bush the size of the province of Utrecht in her garden, so we're making this into an annual tradition. Anyway, wash them and freeze them overnight. If you can't find sloe berries anywhere, blackberries would make a nice alternative.

Divide them between two clean jars and pour the gin over them. Scoop a few spoonfuls of sugar into the gin, close the jars, and shake well so that the sugar mixes and dissolves. Place the jars in a dark spot and forget about them. Shake them sporadically, when you happen to walk by.

After 3 months, or ideally longer, you can pour the gin through a sieve into a clean bottle. Before bottling, taste to see if you like it: If needed, add some sugar. Many recipes for sloe gin are very sweet; I use less sugar to start, as you can always add more. Let the gin stand for another day so the sugar dissolves.

You can gift the bottles or drink it all yourself. Some people pour it into a small glass with lots of ice, but I like it as is, neat, for sipping.

TIP: If your gin is a little cloudy, you can pour it through a cheesecloth-lined sieve.

PINE SYRUP

Makes 2 cups (450 ml)

About 7 ounces (200 g) pine twigs, preferably new growth, but at Christmas we make do with ordinary branches

1 cup (200 g) sugar (the flavor of the sugar—cane sugar, granulated sugar, dark brown sugar—determines the flavor of the syrup, it's your choice)

3 slices fresh ginger (optional)

A few drops of freshly squeezed lemon juice (optional)

A splash of pine syrup is always lovely in a glass of sparkling water with ice, but poured over ice cream, drizzled over a trifle cake, or in a cocktail it can taste very Christmassy.

When you see the ideas on the next page, you'll be making pine syrup until you're ready to drop. So heavenly. It makes for a great gift, by the way: made *from* the tree . . . for *under* the tree.

Rinse the pine branches and cut them into smaller pieces. Strip the needles off the branches or leave them on. The resin taste from the branches is a little stronger than when you only use the needles. You can play around with that. I always use the entire branch.

Put the pine in a saucepan with the sugar, ginger (if using), and ¾ cup plus 1 tablespoon (200 ml) water and place over medium heat. Stir until the sugar is dissolved. Remove from the heat. Cover the pan and allow to steep for a few hours, or preferably an evening or overnight. The longer it steeps, the stronger it will taste.

Strain the syrup through a fine sieve or cheesecloth, season if you wish with a few drops of lemon juice, and keep in a squeaky-clean jar or bottle in the fridge. It will keep for at least a month, or even longer, if you keep the jar clean.

WARNING! Use real pine branches, from your Christmas tree for example. Do not use *yew tree* branches. If you're not certain, Google images for yew. It's a poisonous tree, but it looks like a dark green pine when you squint. The yew tree is the kind of shrub that clutters up boring old gardens, and is quite common, so be alert.

PINE & GINGER DRINK

Makes 1 glass

A handful of pine ice cubes*
3½ tablespoons (50 ml) whiskey
1 tablespoon pine syrup (page 57)
Ginger beer

Fill a rocks glass with pine ice cubes. Pour the whiskey and the pine syrup on top. Top up with ginger beer. Stir briefly.

CHRISTMAS NEGRONI

Makes 1 glass

3½ tablespoons (50 ml) Campari
3½ tablespoons (50 ml) red vermouth
3½ tablespoons (50 ml) gin
5 teaspoons (25 ml) pine syrup (page 57)
4 whole cloves
4 juniper berries, crushed
Plain ice cubes
Pine ice cubes*
1 cinnamon stick

There has to be a negroni recipe in this book, as it's simply my favorite cocktail.

Put the Campari, vermouth, gin, pine syrup, cloves, and juniper berries with some ice in a cocktail shaker and shake firmly, so that the cloves bruise a little.

Strain into a large glass filled with pine ice cubes. Garnish with a cinnamon stick as a stirrer.

CRANBERRY PINE MOCKTAIL

Makes 1 glass

5 or 6 fresh cranberries
Juice of ½ lemon
2 tablespoons pine syrup (page 57)
A few drops of Angostura bitters or bruised orange peel
Pine ice cubes*
Sparkling water

Mix the cranberries, lemon juice, pine syrup, bitters, and a handful of pine ice cubes in a glass. Stir. Top up with sparkling water.

* *Make pine ice cubes in advance by placing a pine twig in each mold in an ice cube tray, filling the molds with water, and freezing them.*

Pine & Ginger Drink

GIN FIZZ WITH BLACKBERRIES

Makes 4 glasses

1 small bunch fresh mint

½ cucumber, sliced

1 scant cup (125 g) blackberries

Juice of 3 limes (about ½ cup plus
    2 tablespoons/150 ml)

2 tablespoons sugar, or more to
    taste

1 cup (250 ml) gin

Lots of crushed ice

2 cups (500 ml) sparkling water

FOR GARNISH

Extra cucumber slices

Blackberries

Lime slices

Sprigs of fresh mint

Put the mint, cucumber, blackberries, lime juice, and sugar in a bowl. With the back of a large wooden spoon, press to bruise everything and to let the juices flow. Pour in the gin and place the bowl in a cool spot to let the flavors marry.

Strain into a pitcher, pressing as much juice out as possible; discard the solids. Divide the marinated gin among four glasses, add ice, and top up with sparkling water. Garnish festively.

ADVOCAAT

(DUTCH EGGNOG)

THIS MAKES FOR A REALLY FUN GIFT

Makes about 4½ cups (1 liter)

12 eggs

1¼ cups (250 g) sugar

Seeds of 1 vanilla bean

1¼ cup plus 2 tablespoons (330 ml) brandy

ALSO NEEDED

A candy thermometer

In a very large metal bowl, beat the eggs with the sugar and vanilla bean until smooth, with a hand mixer fitted with the whisk attachment. Beat in the brandy. Place the bowl on top of a wide saucepan of barely simmering water. Make sure the bowl doesn't touch the water. You can clip a candy thermometer to the bowl if you wish.

With the hand mixer, whisk the egg mixture until it's thick and the thermometer tells you it's about 130°F (54°C) (you can go up to 160°F [70°C], or until it coats the back of a spoon). Never let the *advocaat* get too much hotter than that, or the eggs will scramble. As it heats, it will become foamy, then fluffy and voluminous, then it will collapse and become more fluid just before it reaches the correct temperature.

As soon as the *advocaat* is thick enough, remove the bowl from the pan of hot water and place it in a bowl of cold water. Keep whisking the mixture with a hand mixer at the lowest speed, for about 5 minutes. If there are any lumps, just push the custard through a sieve with a rubber spatula into a clean bowl. Let the *advocaat* cool to room temperature, then pour into a clean covered container and keep in the fridge until ready to use. It will keep for a few weeks in the fridge due to its alcohol content.

Serve the *advocaat* in small glasses or coupes with a small spoon. Or use it in a dessert. A trifle would be great with *advocaat*!

SNACKS

JALAPEÑO DRESSING

PROCESS 10 JALAPEÑOS,
7 TBSP. (100 ML) WHITE
WINE VINEGAR,
SOME SEA SALT,
3 CLOVES OF GARLIC
& ½ CUP (20G)
CHOPPED FRESH
CHIVES
IN A
BLENDER

SERVE WITH
EXTREMELY
FRESH, CREAMY
OYSTERS

GOUGÈRES

Makes 35 gougères

6 tablespoons plus 1 teaspoon
   (90 g) butter, cubed

Freshly grated nutmeg

Sea salt

1 cup (125 g) all-purpose flour

4 eggs

1 heaping cup (125 g) grated
   Gruyère, Comté, or aged Gouda

Freshly ground black pepper

Gougères are small crunchy cheese puffs. They don't even need to be filled, in my opinion. That way you can really taste the delicious cheese. I adore them, especially with a glass of crisp, dry white wine. You can easily store them in an airtight container. Just give them a boost in a hot oven before serving them.

Preheat the oven to 400°F (200°C).

Bring 1 cup (250 ml) water, the butter, nutmeg, and a pinch of salt to a boil in a saucepan, stirring occasionally until the butter has melted. Add the flour and stir with a wooden spoon until smooth. Continue stirring over very low heat until the dough has a nice sheen and comes loose from the sides of the pan.

Remove from the heat. Let cool somewhat.

Beat the eggs in a pitcher and stir them into the flour mixture a splash at a time. Continue until all of the egg has been absorbed; you can use a hand mixer or the spoon as long as you make sure to stir thoroughly. Mix in the cheese, and add pepper to taste.

Fill a pastry bag fitted with a large star tip with the batter. (You can also use two tablespoons to form dollops.) Pipe little mounds on a greased baking sheet with some space between them, as they will expand a bit. Wet your fingertip and smooth the pointy tops.

Bake for 20 minutes, or until golden. Turn off the oven and let them stand in the hot oven for another 5 minutes.

Preferably serve them while still warm, with a glass of wine or a cocktail.

ROASTING SWEET CHESTNUTS

After my mother lit the peat in our fireplace she would place a pan in the smoldering embers to roast the chestnuts that we children had collected outside. Afterward we would dip them in melted Irish butter and sprinkle them with a pinch of sea salt—one of the most delicious things ever.

Use a sharp knife to score an X in the top of each sweet chestnut.

Place the chestnuts in a fireproof bowl (preferably a slotted one to allow the smoky flavor to enter) on the grate of a grill, in a fireplace, or in an oven preheated to 400°F (200°C).

Roast for 10 to 15 minutes. They will burst when done.

Peel them and roll them in melted butter and sprinkle with sea salt.

SPICY GOAT CHEESE SPREAD WITH HOME MADE MELBA TOAST

14 ounces (400 g) fresh goat cheese, at room temperature

3 tablespoons apricot jam

5 peppadew peppers, minced (look for them in the delicatessen section of your supermarket, or jarred in oil)

3 tablespoons minced pickled onion

2 teaspoons spicy mustard

2 tablespoons dry sherry

Sea salt and freshly ground black pepper

FOR THE MELBA TOAST

1 baguette

Prepare

Preheat the oven to 350°F (180°C). Crumble the goat cheese into a thin single layer in a 6-inch (16-cm) broiler-safe baking dish. In a bowl, beat the jam, the peppadews, onion, mustard, and sherry together into a smooth sauce. Season with salt and add a generous grinding of pepper. Spread out over the goat cheese.

Slice the baguette on a diagonal as thinly as possible. Spread the slices out on a baking sheet and toast in the center of the oven for several minutes until brown, flipping halfway through. Stay close, because these will burn easily.

Make

Preheat the broiler to high. Broil the goat cheese for about 5 minutes on a rack in the highest position, until the top bubbles and the edges start browning.

Serve piping hot with the toast as a snack with drinks.

SPICY-SWEET CINNAMON NUTS

3½ cups (500 g) mixed nuts, such as walnuts, cashews, macadamias, pepitas, Brazil nuts, and jumbo peanuts

2 to 3 tablespoons apple syrup

½ cup (125 ml) maple syrup or honey

1 teaspoon cinnamon

Sea salt

1 teaspoon chile flakes (or to taste)

1 tablespoon fresh thyme

Preheat the oven to 350°F (180°C).

Spread the nuts out on a parchment paper–lined baking sheet and bake them in the oven for about 15 minutes, until golden brown and crunchy, flipping them halfway through. Remove them from the oven, but leave the oven on.

In a bowl, combine the apple syrup and maple syrup and stir in the cinnamon, salt to taste, and chile flakes. Stir in the warm nuts until all of them are coated with the syrup.

Spoon them onto the parchment paper–lined baking sheet again. Spread the nuts so they are well separated. Bake for another couple of minutes, until golden brown. Allow them to cool completely. Sprinkle with fresh thyme and break into chunks.

DEEP-FRIED PICKLES WITH BUTTERMILK DIP

FOR THE FRESH BUTTERMILK DIP

¾ cup plus 1 tablespoon (200 ml) sour cream

3½ tablespoons (50 ml) buttermilk

1 small clove garlic, pressed

1 small bunch flat-leaf parsley (½ ounce/15 g), finely chopped

2 tablespoons finely chopped fresh dill

1 tablespoon finely chopped fresh chives

1 tablespoon Worcestershire sauce

1 teaspoon white wine vinegar

Sea salt and freshly ground black pepper to taste

FOR THE DEEP-FRIED PICKLES

1 jar (about 18 ounces/500 g) sweet-sour deli pickles, not too large

About ½ cup plus 2 tablespoons (150 ml) buttermilk

1 tablespoon hot sauce, or a pinch of chile flakes (or to taste)

½ cup (75 g) all-purpose flour

7 tablespoons (75 g) fine polenta or semolina

2 tablespoons paprika (smoked paprika is delicious too!)

1 egg

Sea salt and freshly ground black pepper

Vegetable oil for deep-frying

This is a surprisingly nice drinks snack. After making it at home once, it has become a staple in our bar food repertoire. You simply won't be able to stop eating these. Serve with beer, cava, or dry cider.

Prepare

To make the dip, in a small bowl, combine all the ingredients. Cover and store in the fridge for later use.

Make

Slice the larger pickles lengthwise. Smaller ones you can leave whole. Pat dry with a paper towel.

In a shallow bowl, mix the buttermilk and the hot sauce. Combine the flour, polenta, and paprika in another bowl. Lightly beat the egg and pour it, along with the buttermilk mixture, into the flour mixture. Stir until all lumps have dissolved. The batter should have the consistency of thick yogurt; add a little more buttermilk if needed. Season with salt and pepper. Let stand for a while, allowing it to thicken some more.

In a pan or deep-fryer, heat 2 inches (5 cm) of oil to 350°F (180°C). Dip the pickle slices in batter and fry them in small batches for 2 to 3 minutes, until golden brown and crispy. Drain on paper towels. Serve them hot, with the dip.

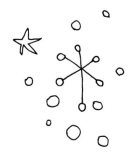

CREAM OF GORGONZOLA & POACHED PEARS ON TOAST

FOR THE POACHED PEAR

5 cooking pears

1¼ cups (300 ml) red wine

1 cinnamon stick

1 star anise

1 strip orange peel

4 tablespoons sugar

Sea salt

FOR THE CREAM

½ cup plus 2 tablespoons
    (150 g) cream cheese, at room
    temperature

9 ounces (250 g) gorgonzola
    cheese, at room temperature

Freshly ground black pepper

FOR SERVING

Nice bread, thinly sliced; you can
    toast it in the oven

Freshly ground black pepper

Coarsely chopped hazelnuts, briefly
    toasted in a dry skillet

Prepare

Peel the pears and put them in a saucepan with the wine, cinnamon stick, star anise, orange peel, sugar, and a pinch of salt. Add enough water to just submerge them. Bring to a boil, then lower the heat and simmer, partially covered, for 30 to 40 minutes, until tender.

Remove the pears from the cooking liquid and let cool. Cut into thick slices and remove the cores if necessary.

Beat the cream cheese with the gorgonzola into a light green cream. Add pepper to taste. Set the cream aside in the fridge to firm up.

Make

Spread a generous dab of cream onto each piece of toast and garnish with a slice of poached pear. Grind some pepper on top and sprinkle with hazelnuts.

On the way home to Amsterdam from Paris: Northern Belgium in the Christmas spirit

SOUPS

LEEK & POTATO CRÈME SOUP WITH FRIED SCALLOPS & PARSLEY OIL

Serves 4

FOR THE SOUP

3 leeks, rinsed and sliced

¼ cup (60 ml) olive oil

1 small clove garlic, minced

1 onion, sliced

4 potatoes, peeled and diced

1 tablespoon curry powder

1 teaspoon freshly grated nutmeg

Sea salt and freshly ground black pepper

1 cup (250 ml) white wine

2 cups (500 ml) vegetable stock

¾ cup plus 1 tablespoon (200 ml) crème fraîche

FOR THE PARSLEY OIL

7 tablespoons (100 ml) mild olive oil

1 small bunch parsley, chopped

Sea salt and freshly ground black pepper

FOR THE SCALLOPS

8 large sea scallops

¼ cup (60 ml) clarified butter

FOR SERVING

3 tablespoons crème fraîche

Prepare

Sauté the leeks in the oil until they're soft, then add the garlic, onion, potatoes, curry powder, and nutmeg and sauté everything briefly. Season with salt and pepper and douse with the wine. Cook over high heat until the wine is reduced, then pour in the stock.

Allow the soup to simmer for 30 minutes. Puree until smooth in a blender or with a hand blender. Stir in the crème fraîche. Set aside.

Make the parsley oil: Put the oil and parsley in the cleaned blender and process for 1 minute, or until smooth. Strain through a fine sieve and season with salt and pepper.

Make

Score the scallops lightly in a diagonal crosshatch pattern.

Heat the clarified butter in a skillet, add the scallops, and cook on both sides until golden brown and just about cooked through.

Meanwhile, reheat the soup in another pan and season with salt and/or pepper, if you wish.

Pour a shallow layer of soup into four deep plates. Make a swirl with a small spoonful of crème fraîche. Place two scallops on top and drizzle with some parsley oil.

PAPAYA GIN GAZPACHO & OYSTERS

Serves about 8

FOR THE SOUP

18 ounces (500 g) papaya, peeled, seeded, and diced

¼ cucumber, peeled and diced

1¼ cups (300 ml) organic tomato juice

Zest of ½ lemon, plus the juice of 1 large lemon

About ½ cup plus 2 tablespoons (150 ml) gin, or to taste

A few drops of Tabasco sauce, or to taste

Sea salt and freshly ground black pepper to taste

A few sprigs of tarragon, plus some for garnish

FOR SERVING

16 oysters (I figure 2 per person; I like Gillardeau, but you might prefer others)

Prepare

Make the soup: Puree all the ingredients in a food processor or blender, taste for seasonings, and refrigerate the gazpacho for at least 1 hour before serving.

Make

Shuck the oysters. With a folded towel, hold an oyster firmly in your hand, with the flat side of the shell facing up. Stick an oyster shucking knife, or a firm, short, and sharp knife, into the hinge, where the two shells come together. You may sometimes have to look for it. Pry between the two halves and carefully stick your knife inside. Slide along the edge of the shell. Twist your knife, so that the shell opens up. Hold the oyster level, to make sure the juices don't run out.

You can throw out the flat shell. Cut the oyster loose from the concave shell. Check for grit and remove it, as it's vile. Pour some liquid out of the shell, and place the open oysters on small plates, or on a big one that's lined with seaweed.

Before serving, pour the soup into glasses. Garnish with some tarragon leaves, sprinkle with salt and pepper, and serve with the oysters on a side plate.

SQUASH CRÈME WITH STAR ANISE & CRAYFISH

Serves 6 to 8

FOR THE SOUP

4 star anise

1 tablespoon grated fresh ginger

1 large onion, diced

Sea salt and freshly ground black
    pepper

2 tablespoons butter

2 tablespoons olive oil

1 teaspoon paprika

Maybe a pinch of cayenne pepper

1 butternut squash (about
    2¼ pounds/1 kg), peeled, seeded,
    and cubed

6½ cups (1.5 liters) vegetable or
    chicken stock

FOR GARNISH

1 tablespoon grated fresh ginger

24 crayfish tails or cocktail shrimps,
    preferably with tails

Sea salt and freshly ground black
    pepper

1 tablespoon olive oil

½ cup plus 2 tablespoons (150 ml)
    crème fraîche, whisked with a
    few drops of pumpkin seed oil,
    plus more pumpkin seed oil

Prepare

Sauté the star anise, ginger, onion, and a generous pinch of salt in the butter and oil in a large heavy pan over medium heat. Cook, stirring occasionally, until the onion is soft, about 10 minutes.

Add the paprika and a pinch of cayenne if you wish. Add the squash cubes and fry them for about 8 minutes, stirring. Pour in the stock. Stir and season the soup with salt and black pepper. Bring to a boil over high heat. When the soup boils, lower the heat and let the soup simmer. Partially cover the pan with a lid. Let the soup simmer for 30 minutes, or until the squash is tender.

Remove the star anise (save it for garnish).

Puree the soup with a hand blender for a long time, at least 7 minutes, until very smooth. This really matters—the longer you do it, the smoother the soup!

This soup can easily be made 2 days in advance: Let it cool to room temperature, then cover and keep it in the fridge.

Make

Toss the ginger with the crayfish tails and let them stand for 30 minutes. Sprinkle with some salt and pepper.

Heat a drop of oil in a nonstick skillet over medium heat and fry the crayfish tails for 2 minutes on each side, stirring continuously.

In the meantime, bring the soup to a boil and divide it among six or eight serving bowls.

Make a swirl with some whipped crème fraîche and place 3 or 4 crayfish tails in each bowl. Drizzle some pumpkin seed oil over it and sprinkle with some pepper. You can garnish with the star anise if you saved them.

PARSNIP APPLE SOUP WITH CURRY, CELERY OIL & SMOKED ALMONDS

Serves 4 to 6

FOR THE CELERY WALNUT OIL

Leaves from 1 bunch celery

⅓ cup (75 ml) walnut oil

⅓ cup (75 ml) mild oil, like sunflower oil, grapeseed oil, or rice bran oil

Sea salt and freshly ground black pepper

About 16 smoked almonds

FOR THE SOUP

2 tablespoons olive oil

3 to 4 parsnips, peeled and diced

2 to 3 potatoes, peeled and diced

1 large onion, diced

2 small cloves garlic, minced

1½ teaspoons curry powder

1½ teaspoons ground coriander

1 teaspoon ground cumin

2 thumbs fresh ginger, finely grated (or 1 teaspoon ground ginger)

6½ cups (1.5 liters) vegetable or chicken stock

1 tart apple (Jonagold, Rome, or Granny Smith), peeled and diced

Sea salt and freshly ground black pepper

Juice of ½ lemon

Prepare

First make the celery walnut oil: Bring a small saucepan of water to a boil. Blanch the celery leaves for 1 minute in the boiling water and scoop them out with a slotted spoon. Let cool and squeeze out the water. Pat dry with a clean dish towel.

Put the squeezed-out celery in a deep container and pour the two oils on top. Season with salt and pepper. Puree with a hand blender until completely smooth. Strain through a fine sieve and discard the solids. Keep in a clean bottle until serving.

Shave the almonds with a fine vegetable slicer, keeping your fingers pressed flat on the almonds. It's relatively easy and provides a flavor and texture very different from plain sliced almonds or chopped smoked almonds. Set aside until ready to serve.

Make the soup: Heat the olive oil in a large saucepan over medium heat. Add the parsnips, potatoes, and onion and sauté until the onion is soft and translucent, about 7 minutes. Stir occasionally. Add the garlic, the spices, and ginger. Sauté for 1 minute.

Add the stock and apple and let the soup simmer for about 20 minutes over low heat until the vegetables are tender.

Puree the soup with a hand blender, or in batches in a regular blender, into a smooth crème. If needed, add salt and pepper and season the soup with lemon juice.

Once it's cooled, keep covered in the fridge until ready to serve, or move on straight away.

Make

Reheat the soup. Divide among four to six bowls. Drizzle the celery oil on top and sprinkle with pepper and the shaved almonds.

BEET SOUP WITH PORT, GOAT CHEESE & SEED CRUNCH BAR

Serves 4

FOR THE SOUP

3 to 4 tablespoons olive oil

1 onion, diced

1 bay leaf

2 small cloves garlic, pressed

2 carrots, peeled and diced

2 ribs celery, diced

18 ounces (500 g) cooked beets, diced

½ cup plus 2 tablespoons (150 ml) red port

2 cups (500 ml) hot vegetable or chicken stock

Sea salt and freshly ground black pepper

About 3 tablespoons freshly squeezed lemon juice

⅓ cup (75 ml) sour cream, whisked

7 ounces (200 g) fresh goat cheese, crumbled

FOR THE SEED CRUNCH BAR

2 small handfuls of seeds: quinoa, hulled pumpkin seeds (pepitas), sesame seeds, poppy seeds, and so on

2 egg whites, beaten

A generous pinch of salt

Doesn't it sound chic, a seed crunch bar? It's super easy, and it has a nice ring to it. And it tastes good, too.

Prepare

Heat the oil in a large heavy saucepan. Add the onion, bay leaf, garlic, carrots, and celery and sauté the vegetables, stirring, for about 5 minutes, until tender.

Add the beets, sauté briefly, and add the port. Stir and add the stock. Let simmer over low heat for 20 minutes. Remove the bay leaf.

With a hand blender, or in batches in a regular blender, puree the soup until completely smooth. Do this for longer than you think necessary, as the longer you puree, the smoother the soup. Season with salt and pepper and add lemon juice to taste. Let cool and keep the soup covered in the fridge until ready to serve.

Make the seed crunch bar: Preheat the oven to 350°F (180°C). Line a baking sheet with parchment paper.

Heat the seeds in a dry skillet until they pop and jump up. Transfer to a bowl and let cool a little. Add the beaten egg whites a little at a time, adding as much as necessary without it becoming too moist. (Or add some more popped seeds.) Season with salt and thinly spread out the seed mixture over the baking sheet.

Bake for 15 minutes, or until crunchy, rotating the baking sheet halfway through for even browning. Break into coarse chunks and keep in an airtight container until ready to serve.

Make

Gently heat the soup. Divide the soup among four deep plates and make a nice swirl in the middle with some sour cream. Crumble the cheese on top and stick in a piece of seed crunch bar. Serve.

Marie in Amsterdam, 2016

Yvette in Saintes-Maries-de-la-Mer, Christmas 2014

WILD MUSHROOM SOUP WITH HAZELNUTS

Serves 4

FOR THE SOUP

1¾ ounces (50 g) dried funghi porcini (cèpes)

3¼ cups (750 ml) warm water

3 shallots, minced

5 tablespoons (75 g) butter

Sea salt and freshly ground black pepper

18 ounces (500 g) wild mushrooms, cleaned

A splash of sherry if you wish

1⅔ cups (400 ml) chicken stock, ideally home made

FOR GARNISH

⅔ cup (75 g) coarsely chopped hazelnuts

A pat of butter

Sea salt and freshly ground black pepper

½ cup (125 ml) crème fraîche, whisked

A few drops of hazelnut oil

Prepare

Steep the dried porcini in the warm water for about 20 minutes, agitating them a bit to dislodge any sand, letting it sink to the bottom. Lift out the reconstituted mushrooms and pour the soaking liquid through a sieve lined with a coffee filter into a container to remove any sand. Finely chop the mushrooms and set them and the liquid aside.

In a large saucepan, sauté the shallots for a few minutes in 1½ tablespoons butter with a pinch of salt. Set about 3½ ounces (100 g) of the prettiest fresh mushrooms aside for garnish and add the remaining fresh mushrooms to the saucepan and sauté them for 5 minutes. Add the chopped porcini and sauté for 1 minute. Add the sherry, if using. Add the reserved soaking water and the stock. Bring everything to a boil and let simmer for about 20 minutes.

Puree the soup with a hand blender, or in batches in a regular blender, until smooth. Add the remaining 3½ tablespoons (50 g) butter and puree for a little longer until you have a nice smooth crème. Season if you wish with salt and pepper.

Make

Just before serving, briefly sauté the reserved fresh mushrooms with the hazelnuts in some butter, and season with salt and pepper.

Reheat the soup until just under a boil—no hotter!—stir thoroughly, and divide among four bowls. Garnish the soup with a lick of crème fraîche, the sautéed mushrooms and nuts, and a drop of hazelnut oil.

CAULIFLOWER CRÈME WITH COCONUT, CUMIN & PINE NUTS

Serves 4

FOR THE CAULIFLOWER CRÈME

2 onions, diced

1 tablespoon olive oil

1 tablespoon butter

2 to 3 small cloves garlic, minced

1 tablespoon toasted cumin seeds, lightly crushed in a mortar

A pinch of cayenne pepper, or to taste

½ teaspoon ground cinnamon

1 head cauliflower, separated into florets

1 (13.5-ounce/400-ml) can coconut milk

2 cups (500 ml) vegetable stock

¾ cup plus 1 tablespoon (200 ml) milk

FOR GARNISH

A small splash of olive oil

2 tablespoons pine nuts, briefly toasted in a dry skillet

A handful of croutons*

Prepare

Sauté the onions in the oil and butter over very low heat in a heavy pan until they are golden brown and sweet, about 20 minutes. Add the garlic, cumin, cayenne, and cinnamon, and stir well. Add the cauliflower and sauté for about 10 minutes over low heat.

Add all the liquids: the coconut milk, stock, and milk. Stir well and place the lid on the pan. Let simmer until the cauliflower is tender, about 20 minutes.

Puree the soup until smooth with a hand blender, and season with some salt and black pepper.

Make

Heat up the soup and ladle it into bowls. Drizzle with a dash of oil, sprinkle with pine nuts and croutons, and serve.

* *Cube day-old bread and arrange it on a parchment paper–lined baking sheet. Drizzle with olive oil and toss with pressed garlic; sprinkle with some salt and freshly ground black pepper, and bake in a 335°F (170°C) preheated oven until cubes are just light brown, about 12 minutes, depending on the size of your croutons. Flip them halfway through for even browning.*

SHRIMP BISQUE & CREAMY ANCHOVY ROUILLE

Serves 4

FOR THE SHRIMP BISQUE

18 ounces (500 g) raw tiger prawns (not peeled; these are available in the frozen seafood section)

¼ cup (60 ml) olive oil, plus extra for frying

1 large onion, diced

2 small cloves garlic, minced

1 large fennel bulb, cored and finely chopped, fronds reserved for garnish

3 large carrots (about 11 ounces/ 300 g), peeled and diced

2 teaspoons paprika

7 tablespoons (100 ml) brandy

1 (14.5-ounce/410-g) can diced tomatoes

4½ cups (1 liter) fish stock

FOR THE CREAMY ANCHOVY ROUILLE

1 roasted sweet red pepper, from a jar

7 tablespoons (100 ml) mayonnaise

1 slice white bread (or 2 slices baguette)

2 anchovy fillets, finely chopped

2 teaspoons Dijon mustard, or to taste

Juice of ½ lemon, or to taste

2 small cloves garlic, minced

¼ cup (60 ml) olive oil

Sea salt and freshly ground black pepper

A drop of Tabasco sauce, or to taste

Prepare

Peel each prawn: Pull of its head and then grab the legs to pull away its shell; reserve the shell. Remove the bowels (the black vein) on its back with a paring knife. Set aside 8 prawns, the prettiest, covered in the fridge, for garnish.

Heat the oil in a large saucepan and fry the prawn shells for about 5 minutes, stirring. Add the onion, garlic, fennel, carrot, and paprika and fry everything for 10 minutes, or until the vegetables are tender. Douse with the brandy and cook for another 2 minutes, until the alcohol has evaporated somewhat. Add the tomatoes and stock and let the soup simmer for 30 minutes. Add the peeled prawns for the final 5 minutes and simmer until cooked through.

In two batches, puree the soup in a blender until completely smooth. Puree for a good long while; it should be as smooth as possible. Give it more time than you think is necessary. Pour the smooth pureed soup through a sieve that you've placed over a clean saucepan and press the soup through with the back of a wooden spoon. Discard grit or shells that stay behind. Thin the soup with a dash of water or stock if you find it too thick. Let the soup cool, cover, and refrigerate until ready to serve.

Puree all the ingredients for the rouille in the cleaned blender to a smooth sauce. Taste to see if it needs more lemon juice, Tabasco, or mustard, and finish the sauce to your own preference. It doesn't need to be too thick. Later on you'll stir it into the soup.

Make

Heat the soup.

Fry the reserved prawns on both sides in some oil, for 2 minutes max.

Ladle the soup into nice deep plates, swirl the rouille in the soup, and garnish with the fried prawns and the fennel fronds. Grind some pepper over the soup and serve.

SMALL PLATES

TERRINE OF WILD RABBIT & PISTACHIOS

1 wild rabbit, deboned (14 to 18 ounces/400 to 500 g meat) (available throughout most of the year—you can also buy farm raised, but wild rabbit has a little more flavor)

1 tablespoon juniper berries

3 dried bay leaves

14 ounces (400 g) chicken livers

14 ounces (400 g) bacon (or more if not using caul fat)

3½ tablespoons (50 ml) cognac

3½ tablespoons (50 ml) dry sherry

4 small cloves garlic, minced

A pinch of freshly grated nutmeg

2 teaspoons fresh thyme

Heaping ½ teaspoon (3 g) curing salt

1¼ teaspoons regular (kosher) salt

A pinch of freshly ground black pepper

2 eggs, beaten

⅔ cup (75 g) shelled pistachios

A knob of butter for greasing the baking pans

A piece of pork caul fat (crépinette) or an additional 11 ounces (300 g) bacon, cut into thin strips

ON THE SIDE

Onion-ginger compote, horseradish mustard, or tart beets (pages 258–59)

A terrine is a pâté that is made in a . . . wait for it: terrine, a ceramic dish that conducts heat evenly. Traditionally a pâté is baked in a dough crust. In French the word *pâte* means "dough," but these days the official names have become somewhat mixed up. In France a pâté baked in a crust is now referred to as a *pâté en croûte*, which you could argue is in fact redundant. But because I like to do things the formal way for this occasion, I will call my pâté a "terrine."

Although I use a terrine mold for this recipe, you could just as easily use a loaf pan or a baking dish. This recipe is freely based on a recipe given to me by my friend Floris Brester, who in his Pasteibakkerij shop in Amsterdam creates the most beautiful and delicious pâtés.

Ask your butcher to debone a rabbit for you or do it yourself. In general a wild rabbit will yield 14 to 18 ounces (400 to 500 g) of meat. Cut the larger pieces (the thighs, for example) into smaller cubes and set them aside (those should be about one-third of the meat).

Use a pestle and mortar to pulverize the juniper berries and bay leaves.

Mince the rest of the rabbit meat, the chicken livers, and bacon in a food processor—or, if you have one, a meat grinder with the coarse die. Spoon everything into a bowl and add the reserved larger rabbit chunks, as well as the cognac, sherry, garlic, nutmeg, thyme, curing salt, kosher salt, pepper, and eggs. Make sure your hands are spotless before using them to combine everything. Give it a good kneading, until the meat mixture becomes quite sticky. At the end, mix in the pistachios.

Cover and let marinate for about 2 hours, or, better, in the fridge over-night, allowing the individual ingredients to get well acquainted.

Butter two or three ceramic terrine molds or small loaf pans (total volume about 6½ cups/1.5 liters) and line them with strips of bacon or the pork caul fat, laying them inside the molds like a hammock, with plenty of overhang.

Spoon in the rabbit mixture, carefully pressing down to make sure no air pockets are left. Fold the caul fat over the top or place a layer of bacon on top to cover the rabbit mixture. Cover with a lid or parchment paper. Wrap the entire terrine mold in aluminum foil.

Preheat the oven to 250°F (120°C).

Place the terrines on a rimmed baking sheet or oven tray to collect the drips of escaping fat and bake for 2 hours.

Remove the lid and continue baking for another 20 to 30 minutes, giving your pâté a nice brown color. Allow to cool, then store your pâté in the fridge for at least 1 day, but preferably a couple more. This will allow the flavors to fully develop. Slice and serve with one or more of the accompaniments.

TERRINE OF TENDER LEEK WITH SMOKED SALMON & MASCARPONE

10 medium-size or 6 large leeks

1 (¼-ounce) envelope unflavored gelatin powder, or 2 gelatin sheets

8 ounces (225 g) mascarpone

1 cup (230 g) cream cheese, at room temperature

Sea salt and freshly ground black pepper

7 ounces (200 g) smoked wild salmon

1 generous bunch fresh chives

This is a wonderful starter that you can make in advance even for large dinner parties. If you don't eat fish, leave out the salmon or replace it with vegetables cooked al dente. Think: peas, fava beans, or carrots—also great!

Prepare

Preheat the oven to 400°F (200°C).

Line a 1-quart (1-liter) terrine mold or a 9 by 5-inch (23 by 12-cm) loaf pan with plastic wrap, with a generous overhang around the edges.

Trim the root end and the dark green tops off the leeks. If they're very large, cut them in half lengthwise. Rinse them very thoroughly until all sand has been washed off. Place them on a parchment paper–lined baking sheet. Roast the leeks for about 30 minutes, or until brown and very tender. Let cool.

If using powdered gelatin, sprinkle it over ¼ cup (60 ml) cold water in a cup and let stand until softened, 5 to 10 minutes. (Soak gelatin sheets in a bowl of cold water until softened, then drain and squeeze out the excess water.)

In a saucepan, heat the mascarpone over low heat, stirring, then add the soaked gelatin and stir to dissolve. Immediately remove the pan from the heat and beat in the cream cheese. Generously season with salt and pepper.

Peel off and discard the leeks' outermost layers so only the soft cores remain. Use the widest leaves to line the bottom and sides of the terrine mold; press them a little to flatten if necessary, overlapping them slightly, like roof tiles. Allow the ends to hang over the edge a little.

Spread one-third of the mascarpone mixture on top of this bottom layer and cover with leeks, a layer of salmon, and whole chives. Repeat with another third of the mascarpone and continue layering until you have used up all the ingredients. Fold over the overhanging leek leaves and then cover with the plastic wrap. Place in the fridge to firm up at least 8 hours or overnight.

Make

Remove the terrine from the fridge about 1 hour before serving. Unfold the plastic covering the top and invert the terrine onto a cutting board. Lift off the mold and remove the rest of the plastic wrap. Use a sharp, warm knife to cut your terrine into gorgeous slices. Arrange them on a platter, sprinkle with crushed peppercorns if you wish, and serve.

MUSHROOM TARTLETS WITH GOAT CHEESE & BEETS

½ (17.3-ounce/490-g) box frozen puff pastry dough (1 sheet), thawed

2 to 3 cooked beets, quartered

3 tablespoons raspberry vinegar

Sea salt and freshly ground black pepper

6 tablespoons (90 ml) olive oil

18 ounces (500 g) wild mushrooms, cleaned and shredded into large pieces

Several fresh thyme and sage leaves, plus some extra for garnish

10½ ounces (300 g) fresh spinach, washed

⅔ cup (75 g) crumbled soft goat cheese

Prepare

Preheat the oven to 350°F (180°C).

Cut the puff pastry dough into four squares and place them on a parchment paper–lined baking sheet. Use a sharp knife to score a square into each sheet, about ⅜ inch (1 cm) from the edges, creating "picture frames." Perforate the inner square with a fork. Bake for 15 to 20 minutes, until nicely golden brown. If the perforated middle part has risen as well, cut it away with a knife so you have little pastry boxes. Set these crusts aside.

Sprinkle the beets with the vinegar and a pinch of salt and pepper and cover until ready to serve.

Heat 2 tablespoons of the oil in a large skillet and add the mushrooms; sauté for about 8 minutes, until all the liquid has evaporated from the pan. While cooking, add the thyme and sage. In another pan, use the remaining oil to sauté the spinach over high heat until wilted. Season with salt and pepper. Drain the spinach well. Set everything aside.

Make

Preheat the oven to 350°F (180°C).

Divide the mushroom mixture, spinach, and beets among the four puff pastry crusts. Sprinkle the goat cheese on top. Bake for 15 to 20 minutes, until the cheese is melted. Garnish with fresh herbs and serve.

PORTOBELLO & PEAR SALAD

Serves 6 to 8

8 large portobello mushrooms, stems removed

Sea salt and freshly ground black pepper

3½ tablespoons (50 ml) olive oil

2 tablespoons balsamic vinegar

1 small clove garlic, minced

2 tablespoons freshly squeezed lemon juice

1 teaspoon chopped fresh thyme

3 Doyenné du Comice pears, extremely thinly sliced and sprinkled with a splash of lemon juice to prevent discoloration

4 heads Little Gem lettuce, leaves separated, large ones torn in half

1 cucumber, thinly sliced

A small handful of flat-leaf parsley, coarsely chopped

About ½ cup (50 g) thinly shaved Parmesan cheese

Prepare

Heat a grill pan until piping hot.

Sprinkle the gills of each mushroom with salt and pepper. Grill them, gills facing up, over medium heat until well done: After about 10 minutes you will see little drops forming inside the mushrooms; they will tenderize in their own liquid while staying firm and flavorful. Continue cooking for a couple of minutes until you think they are done. Store them, gills facing up, on a covered plate until ready to serve.

In a dish, combine the oil, vinegar, garlic, lemon juice, and thyme. Season with salt and pepper. Set the dressing aside.

Make

Put the pear, lettuce, cucumber, and parsley in a bowl, sprinkle two-thirds of the dressing on top, and toss everything together using a spoon.

Cut the mushrooms into strips.

Divide the salad among six to eight plates. Top with the mushrooms. Sprinkle with the cheese and the rest of the dressing. Serve straightaway.

MINI BRIE & WHISKEY COCOTTES WITH RAISINS & VANILLA

FOR THE WHISKEY COCOTTES

½ cup plus 2 tablespoons (150 ml) whiskey (or brandy)

4 tablespoons raisins

Seeds of 1 vanilla bean

1 (10½-ounce/300-g) wheel of brie, rind removed, diced

Freshly ground black pepper

FOR SERVING

Nice artisanal breadsticks

Belgian endive leaves and chopped pear or cooked and halved new potatoes

Prepare

In a saucepan, heat the whiskey with the raisins and vanilla. When it's just about to boil, remove from the heat and let stand for 30 minutes.

Divide the raisins among four individual casseroles or mini cocottes, reserving a few for garnish. Divide the brie into four equal portions and place these on top of the raisins. Pour the whiskey over the cheese. Grind black pepper on top. Set aside.

Make

Preheat the oven to 400°F (200°C).

Bake the cocottes for about 20 minutes, until the cheese is soft. If the top isn't browned after 20 minutes, turn on the broiler and broil until golden brown. Scatter the reserved raisins over the brie.

Serve each cocotte on a plate lined with a napkin so it won't slide. Serve with the breadsticks and the endives, and some pieces of pear or cooked baby potatoes on a skewer.

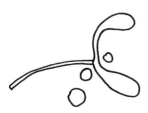

POTATO PATTIES
WITH CRAB RÉMOULADE

FOR THE POTATO PATTIES

3 potatoes (about 9 ounces/250 g)
    or leftover mashed potato from
    an earlier Christmas dinner

¾ cup plus 1 tablespoon (100 g)
    self-rising flour*

A pinch of salt

Butter for cooking

FOR THE MAYONNAISE

*Make sure that all ingredients are at
    room temperature*

1 tablespoon spicy mustard

Juice of ½ lemon

1 egg yolk

About ½ cup plus 2 tablespoons
    (150 ml) light vegetable oil

1 teaspoon horseradish (from a jar)

A pinch of smoked paprika

Sea salt and freshly ground black
    pepper

FOR THE CRAB SALAD

10½ ounces (300 g) celeriac,
    peeled

7 ounces (200 g) crabmeat (fresh
    or canned)

2 Granny Smith apples

Freshly squeezed lemon juice

A handful of arugula or 1 bunch
    watercress, tough stems
    removed

About ½ cup (25 g) fresh flat-leaf
    parsley leaves

And maybe some peppergrass or
    some nice corn salad leaves

Prepare

Cook the potatoes until tender, peel and mash them (preferably with a potato ricer). Mix in the self-rising flour and salt and briefly knead to make a coherent dough. Roll out into a thick log. Wrap in plastic and refrigerate until ready to cook.

Make the mayo: Combine the mustard, lemon juice, and egg yolk. While beating with a hand blender, pour in half of the oil in a slow trickle until you get a creamy mayonnaise. Season with horseradish, smoked paprika, and salt and pepper, and add just enough extra oil so that your mayonnaise reaches the desired consistency.

For the crab salad, coarsely grate the celeriac with a grater or mandoline, or use a food processor. Spoon in 3 generous tablespoons of the mayonnaise. Place the celeriac salad—which is now called rémoulade—and the mayonnaise in the fridge until ready to serve.

Make

Heat a little butter in a nonstick pan. Cut the potato log into thin slices. Briefly fry the slices on both sides until golden brown. Make one or two patties per person, depending on the diameter of your roll. Keep them warm on a plate in the oven set to the lowest temperature.

Meanwhile, finish the crab salad: If you use canned crab, make sure to thoroughly drain it first. Slice the apples into matchsticks, leaving the skin on. Sprinkle with some lemon juice to prevent discoloration. Mix the crab, apples, the rémoulade, and if needed some extra mayonnaise together.

Divide the potato patties among serving plates and arrange the salad on top or to the side using a ring mold or a cookie cutter. Garnish with a fresh herb salad of arugula, parsley, and whatever you happen to have on hand— perhaps some peppergrass or something like that.

---

* *To make your own self-rising flour, combine ½ cup (110 g) cake flour, 1 teaspoon (5 g) baking powder, and ½ teaspoon salt.*

VICTOR'S CRAYFISH COCKTAIL

Serves 4

2 tablespoons mayonnaise

2 tablespoons ketchup

1 tablespoon whiskey

1 tablespoon horseradish (from a jar)

1 tablespoon Worcestershire sauce

Juice of 2 lemons, plus 1 sliced lemon

2 heads Little Gem lettuce, cut into thin strips

1 small fennel bulb, peeled and exceptionally thinly shaved, fronds reserved for garnish

Leaves from 3 sprigs fresh tarragon, plus some extra sprigs for garnish

Sea salt and freshly ground black pepper

7 tablespoons (100 ml) heavy cream

A pinch of salt

A pinch of cayenne pepper

A pinch of chili powder, or to taste

FOR ON TOP

9 ounces (250 g) cooked and peeled crayfish tails

Paprika, chile flakes, or piment d'Espelette

Let's eat crayfish instead of shrimp more often. They have become a real nuisance in our local waters—and besides, they are delicious! These days you can buy them in most good supermarkets, peeled and ready.

These cocktails used to be my father's favorite starter. Often, when we had something to celebrate, he would prepare them for us. So this is pretty much his recipe. In my mind I can still see his face lighting up the moment he began digging in. He would, by the way, never wait for the others to start eating. He simply loved this dish too much.

If you decide to use shrimp instead of crayfish, use Dutch shrimp, those small gray ones, if you can find them. They are wonderful. Otherwise just use the freshest shrimp available.

This dish may sound a bit old-fashioned. But let's be honest: When you have both young and old gathering at your dinner table, wouldn't you prefer to see only happy faces all around?

Prepare

Mix the mayonnaise, ketchup, whiskey, horseradish, Worcestershire sauce, and 1 tablespoon lemon juice and set aside in the fridge until ready to serve.

No more than an hour in advance, combine the lettuce, fennel, and tarragon. Toss with the remaining lemon juice and season with salt and pepper. Cover and refrigerate.

Make

Whip the cream, and when soft peaks begin to form, add some salt and cayenne. Fold in the mayo-ketchup mixture. Season the creamy cocktail sauce with some chili powder.

Divide the fennel salad among four wide cocktail glasses. Put almost all of the crayfish on top and spoon a generous dollop of cocktail sauce into each of the four glasses. Top with the remaining crayfish.

Garnish the cocktails with those lemon slices, tarragon sprigs, and reserved fennel fronds. Sprinkle with paprika, chili flakes, or some piment d'Espelette.

RABBIT (OR CHICKEN) RILLETTES

Serves 8

3 rabbit legs (or chicken thighs)

Sea salt and freshly ground black pepper

3½ tablespoons (50 g) butter

3½ tablespoons (50 ml) olive oil

A few sprigs fresh thyme

1 cup (250 ml) white wine

About ½ cup (125 ml) crème fraîche

3 tablespoons chopped fresh tarragon

Juice and finely grated zest of at least ½ lemon, or to taste

FOR SERVING

Crusty bread, a nice baguette, or toast

Possibly some cornichons (small French pickles)

Of course the name technically isn't correct: In French cuisine, rillettes are traditionally made from fatty meat trimmings: pork or goose, for instance. The meat is slow cooked in its own fat, after which it solidifies into a much-beloved, spreadable rustic paste. Rabbit and chicken are relatively lean. Therefore I add some fat myself: The crème fraîche provides the requisite creaminess in this recipe, making it a bizarrely delicious little starter that you can make in advance and store in the fridge. Lovely.

Prepare

Sprinkle the rabbit legs with salt and pepper. Heat the butter and oil in a heavy-bottomed pan. Brown the rabbit on all sides. Add the thyme. Douse with the wine and cover with a lid. Lower the heat and let the rabbit stew for about 2 hours, until the meat starts to loosen from the bones. Check once in a while to make sure the pan isn't too dry, and pour in a splash of wine or water if needed. Flip the meat now and again.

Allow the meat to cool somewhat without letting it get too cold. With clean hands, pull all the meat from the bones and remove the thyme sprigs. Keep the fat in the pan!

Shred the meat in a stand mixer or hand mixer using the whisk attachment; do not use a knife or food processor. If you grind the meat in a food processor you'll end up with baby food, and that's not what I have in mind. The meat's texture shouldn't be broken down.

Add the crème fraîche as well as some of the reduced wine-fat mixture from the pan. Season the rillettes with salt, pepper, tarragon, and the lemon zest and juice. You may be a little bold. Otherwise they can become too bland after cooling down.

Transfer to small clean jars or a spotless bowl and store the rillettes in the fridge to stiffen. This can be done a few days in advance.

Make

Remove the rillettes from the fridge several hours before serving so they won't be ice-cold and will be smooth and spreadable. Give each dinner guest a mini jar, or a generous scoop on each plate, along with some bread and cornichons.

Fresh air on Boxing Day, 2016

Rudolph: the Prehistoric Elk, Temple House, County Sligo, Ireland

ROASTED KOHLRABI WITH CHANTERELLES & RYE BREADCRUMBS

Serves 4

FOR THE ROASTED KOHLRABI

4 cups (500 g) all-purpose flour

6½ tablespoons (100 g) sea salt

1 large kohlrabi, or 2 smaller ones, not peeled, leaves removed (or use rutabaga)

FOR THE DISH

1 slice dark Frisian rye bread

2 handfuls small chanterelles (or another delicious type of mushroom), cleaned, the larger ones shredded to the size of the smaller ones

2 to 3 tablespoons olive oil, plus 2 to 3 tablespoons for garnish

Sea salt and freshly ground black pepper

A knob of butter

About 1¾ ounces (50 g) Parmesan or Pecorino, very thinly shaved

About 4 fresh sage leaves, very thinly sliced

3 to 4 tablespoons white balsamic or cider vinegar

Prepare

Preheat the oven to 400°F (200°C).

Make a dough from the flour, salt, and about ¾ cup (200 ml) water. Knead with clean hands into a firm, somewhat spongy dough, adding a little more water or flour if needed. Roll out on a floured countertop. Wrap the dough around the kohlrabi, making sure all the seams have been carefully sealed tight. If needed, use a splash of cold water to make them stick together easier.

Place the dough-wrapped kohlrabi on a baking sheet and bake for 2 hours.

Use a hammer or a cleaver to tap open the dough ball (beware: hot steam!) and carefully remove the roasted kohlrabi from its housing—use pliers if necessary. Wipe the kohlrabi clean and let it cool off a little.

Slice the kohlrabi as thinly as possible, cover, and set aside or, if you are doing this more than 3 hours in advance, refrigerate. If refrigerating, don't forget to remove the slices in advance to let them come to room temperature before serving.

Grind the rye bread into coarse breadcrumbs in the food processor. Set aside.

Make

Sauté the chanterelles in olive oil until tender, seasoning with salt and pepper. Drain on paper towels.

Put some butter in a skillet and, while stirring, fry the breadcrumbs for a few minutes, until crunchy. Drain on paper towels. Spread the thinly sliced kohlrabi on nice large serving plates. Scatter the mushrooms over the slices and sprinkle with cheese shavings, sage, and vinegar. Add a splash of olive oil. Sprinkle with the breadcrumbs. Grind some black pepper on top and serve.

MACKEREL TARTLET

Serves 6

FOR THE SHORT-CRUST DOUGH

2⅓ cups (300 g) all-purpose flour

A pinch of salt

½ teaspoon paprika

10½ tablespoons (150 g) cold
    butter, cubed

1 egg

A few drops of ice-cold milk

FOR THE FILLING

3 eggs

1 cup (250 ml) crème fraîche

1 cup (100 g) grated aged cheese

2 tablespoons finely chopped fresh
    dill

½ tablespoon paprika

Sea salt and freshly ground black
    pepper

7 ounces (200 g) smoked mackerel
    fillet, chopped

This is a useful dish that serves six to eight people. Because you can serve this tart cold, the recipe can be completed in advance. Serve with a salad of arugula, watercress, and fresh garden herbs dressed with some vinegar and olive oil.

Prepare

Make the short-crust dough: Combine the flour, salt, and paprika. Using cool hands, swiftly knead in the butter, followed by the egg. Add enough drops of milk to make a coherent dough. Wrap in plastic and refrigerate for 1 hour so the dough can rest.

Preheat the oven to 350°F (180°C).

Roll out the dough on a floured countertop and press it into a greased pie pan about 9½ inches (24 cm) in diameter. Carefully trim the edges. Line the crust with parchment paper, fill with pie weights or dried beans, and blind bake the crust for 15 minutes.

Remove the weights and parchment, bake the crust for another 5 minutes, then let the crust cool for a while on a rack. Leave the oven on.

Beat the eggs together with the crème fraîche. Stir in half of the cheese, the dill, and paprika. Season with salt and pepper to taste.

Spread the mackerel on the blind-baked crust. Pour in the egg mixture and sprinkle the rest of the cheese on top. Bake the tart for 25 to 30 minutes, until it turns light brown and the egg has solidified. Let cool.

Make

Serve in slices with a salad on the side.

BEETS, SMOKED CURD & ROASTED BUCKWHEAT

Serves 6 to 8

FOR THE CURD

4½ cups (1 liter) plain yogurt

Zest and juice of 1 lemon

Sea salt and freshly ground black pepper

FOR THE SALAD

8 beets (a mix of colors would be nice, of course!)

3 tablespoons olive oil

2 tablespoons whole buckwheat groats

Zest of 1 lemon

FOR THE WHEY DRESSING

About 5 tablespoons (75 ml) whey from the yogurt (can be replaced with freshly squeezed lemon juice)

Sea salt and freshly ground black pepper

½ cup (120 ml) hazelnut oil or light olive oil

ALSO NEEDED

A smoker box (you can easily make one yourself: see page 151)

2 tablespoons smoking chips

Curd is the most basic fresh cheese that you can make yourself without the use of rennet or other additives. It's not widely available in stores, but making it is so uncomplicated that you should definitely try to do so yourself. Just remember to begin a day in advance! The yogurt needs to drain overnight. Briefly smoke the curd, and you won't believe just how wonderful it will taste.

Prepare

Place a clean dish towel in a strainer. Place the strainer over a large bowl. Pour in the yogurt and cover with plastic wrap. Set aside in the basement, the fridge, or in another cool spot in the house. The next day, stir the zest and juice into the strained yogurt and season with salt and pepper. Save some of the whey that drained into the bowl for your dressing!

Preheat the oven to 400°F (200°C).

Put the beets in an olive oil–greased baking dish, sprinkle with another splash of oil, and cover with aluminum foil. Bake the beets for at least 1 hour, until you can easily pierce them with a sharp knife. Let cool somewhat and rub off the peels. Cover and refrigerate until ready to serve.

Make the whey dressing: Put the whey in a bowl. Add salt and pepper and stir with a small whisk until the salt has dissolved. Continue whisking while adding the oil. Cover and refrigerate.

Put the curd in a small bowl. Fill one side of the smoker box with the wood chips and put the bowl on the rack on the other side of the box. Cover and smoke for 2 minutes over low heat.

Remove from the heat and leave the curd inside the smoker for another 5 minutes. Spoon into a pastry bag or cover the bowl and refrigerate until ready to serve.

Toast the buckwheat in a dry skillet until the grains pop. Set aside.

Make

Slice the cooked beets as thinly as possible. The easiest way to do this is on a Japanese mandoline or a vegetable slicer. Divide the beet slices among six to eight plates. Drizzle with three-quarters of the dressing and allow it to absorb—it should steep for at least 30 minutes.

Spoon or pipe fat dollops of the smoked curd onto the beets. Sprinkle with black pepper and the roasted buckwheat. Grate some lemon zest on top and serve straightaway.

SMOKED CHICKEN SALAD WITH GRAPES & PARMESAN-TARRAGON DRESSING

Serves 4

FOR THE DRESSING

7 tablespoons (100 g) plain Greek yogurt (10% fat)

½ cup (50 g) finely grated Parmesan cheese

3 tablespoons home made mayonnaise (page 269)

2 tablespoons white wine vinegar

1½ teaspoons dried tarragon

Sea salt and freshly ground black pepper

FOR THE SALAD

1 small fennel bulb, very thinly shaved, fronds reserved for garnish

2 heads Belgian endive, cut into thin strips

Juice of 1 lemon

1 container vegetable sprouts, such as red cabbage or radish sprouts (alfalfa and garden cress are great too)

A handful of seedless white grapes, halved

6 tablespoons (50 g) shelled pistachios, coarsely chopped

2 smoked chicken breasts (or smoked trout fillet!), cut into strips

I'm a big proponent of fresh herbs, but sometimes the dried variety has a completely different flavor from the fresh one. Dried oregano, for example, has a taste all its own, one that lends itself better to certain recipes. Or take fresh cilantro and dried coriander seeds: They taste totally dissimilar!

The same goes for tarragon: Fresh tarragon tastes like fresh licorice or anise, while the taste of dried tarragon is much richer—almost creamy! This is precisely why it works so well in this dressing. I wholeheartedly recommend it. Besides, during the middle of winter it's a godsend, because that's when there's no fresh tarragon to be found on my terrace.

Prepare

In a large bowl, whisk the yogurt, cheese, mayonnaise, vinegar, tarragon, and salt and pepper to make a dressing. Refrigerate until ready to serve.

Place the shaved fennel in a bowl of ice water and let stand for 20 minutes, or until it becomes crunchy and starts to curl a little.

Toss the Belgian endive with the lemon juice in a large bowl.

Make

Drain the fennel and spin it dry in a clean kitchen towel or a salad spinner. Add to the endive, along with the sprouts, grapes, and pistachios, and toss. Divide the salad among four wide glass cups. Drizzle with the dressing, arrange the chicken strips and reserved fennel fronds on top, and serve.

VEGETARIAN RUSSIAN POTATO SALAD

Serves 6

FOR THE SALAD

1¾ pounds (800 g) firm cooking potatoes, peeled, larger ones halved

5 carrots, peeled

3 cups (400 g) frozen shelled green peas

¼ cup (40 g) minced pickled onions or cornichons

1 red onion, finely diced

1 tart apple, finely diced

FOR THE SAUCE

1 tablespoon coarse mustard

1 tablespoon fine mustard

6 tablespoons (90 ml) home made mayonnaise (page 269)

3 tablespoons crème fraîche

½ bunch fresh flat-leaf parsley, finely chopped

Sea salt and freshly ground black pepper to taste

FOR THE GARNISH

About 2 heads Little Gem lettuce

4 to 5 hard-boiled eggs, peeled and quartered

6 small sour pickles or cornichons

Freshly ground black pepper

Restaurant Rijsel in Amsterdam is always packed, not just because of their excellent service, heavenly wine selection, and famous baked potatoes, but most of all because of their delicious Russian potato salad, which you can order as a starter. This lowly salad is everyone's guilty pleasure. When buying it at a gas station many of us tend to obscure our container of Russian potato salad with a newspaper and a bottle of mineral water. But in this restaurant you can be up front about it.

Now, I'm going to flat-out profess my love for the Russian salad. Of course it traditionally contains cold meat stew or ham, but since we want to keep everyone at the table happy, I will omit the meat here. Just as delicious. In the end it's all about the generous dollop of home made mayo.

Thanks to Chef Iwan, who decided to place this salad on the menu, and told me that it quite simply is a top dish that should be a staple on every holiday dinner table.

Prepare

Cook the potatoes in boiling water until al dente, about 20 minutes, adding the carrots after 10 minutes and the peas after 15 minutes because they need to cook only very briefly. Drain, rinse with cold water, and let cool. Cut the potatoes into small cubes and the carrots into thin slices. Mix with all the other ingredients for the salad.

Combine the ingredients for the sauce and add several dollops of sauce to the salad, making it smooth and creamy. Save the remaining sauce for serving.

You can finish the Russian potato salad now or cover and refrigerate for later use.

Make

Spoon one scoop of potato salad onto each plate and garnish with the lettuce leaves and hard-boiled eggs. Pour some extra sauce over the salad and garnish with a cornichon. Sprinkle with pepper and serve.

MAIN COURSES

WHOLE SIDE OF SALMON WITH FENNEL, LEMON & WATERCRESS-MISO MAYO

Serves at least 6

1 lemon, extremely thinly sliced

1 fennel bulb, extremely thinly sliced, fronds chopped

2 to 3 tablespoons olive oil

1 whole (wild Alaskan) side of salmon (2¼ pounds/1 kg)

Sea salt

A splash of white wine

2 teaspoons pink peppercorns, crushed, or freshly ground four-seasons peppercorns

ON THE SIDE

Watercress-miso mayo (page 269)

This is an incredibly easy—but at the same time not unimpressive—dish. Delicious with some steamed potatoes and salad. I urge you to cook the salmon very briefly; the surface should be nearly raw, although just warm enough. Overcooked salmon is dry, boring, and therefore a waste. You will immediately recognize the moment of going "too far" when you see white solidified protein appearing on the surface. Since you are cooking an entire side of salmon that is uneven in thickness, you'll cover the flatter and thinner tail end with slices of fennel and cook the salmon only briefly. You'll be all right.

Prepare

Make sure that all the ingredients are ready: the sliced lemon and fennel in one bowl, the fennel fronds in a separate bowl. Store in the fridge until ready to use.

Make the mayo. You can find a good recipe on page 269. If you use mayo from a jar instead, stir in some lemon juice for extra freshness. Refrigerate until ready to use.

Make

Preheat the oven to 350°F (180°C). Line a baking sheet with two amply overlapping sheets of aluminum foil with plenty of overhang. Place a sheet of parchment paper on the foil.

Brush the parchment with oil and place the salmon on top. Sprinkle with salt and divide the lemon and fennel slices over the fish. Sprinkle with the wine and pink peppercorns.

Place another sheet of parchment paper on top and cover with the foil. Thoroughly seal the edges so nothing will leak out.

Place the baking sheet in the oven and bake for 18 to 20 minutes, until the internal temperature reaches 125°F (50°C) at most.

Serve the salmon whole, sprinkled with the fennel fronds, and serve the mayo in a bowl on the side.

MINCEMEAT-STUFFED PHEASANTS WITH BRANDY SAUCE

Serves 4 to 6

2 (1¾-pound/800-g) pheasant hens, or 1 (2¼-pound/1-kg) pheasant rooster

2 tablespoons butter, softened

Sea salt and freshly ground black pepper

A pinch of freshly grated nutmeg

1 cup plus 2 tablespoons (250 g) mincemeat (page 261)

Leaves from 2 sprigs fresh rosemary, chopped

A handful of fresh breadcrumbs

8 to 10 slices bacon

A glass of brandy or cognac, plus more to taste

Depending on the weight of the pheasant, one bird will suffice for three or four people. For four to six diners, get two hens, to be safe. One rooster serves just about four.

Pheasant goes great with sauerkraut, of course; serve with roast potatoes and stuffed apples (page 174) and the mashed potato and celeriac with apple found on page 176.

Prepare

Rub the pheasant with half of the butter and sprinkle it inside and out with salt, pepper, and nutmeg.

Combine the mincemeat with the rosemary and breadcrumbs and use the mixture to stuff the pheasant.

Over high heat, fry the bacon for a couple of minutes in a heavy-bottomed pan—one that is oven safe and has a lid—until nearly crispy. Drain on a paper towel. Now brown the pheasant on all sides in the bacon fat.

Arrange the strips of bacon, overlapping like roof tiles, on top of the pheasant and neatly tie everything together with kitchen twine. Return the pheasant to the pan and cover with a lid. Refrigerate until ready to roast.

Make

Allow the pheasant to sit at room temperature for about 30 minutes.

Preheat the oven to 335°F (170°C).

Pour a glass of brandy over the pheasant. Cover the pan with a lid and roast in the oven for 50 to 60 minutes, until cooked through. Remove the pheasant from the pan and let rest underneath a sheet of aluminum foil.

Douse the pan with a splash of water and a few tablespoons brandy, and let boil for a while until everything that's stuck to the pan has come loose. Reduce the heat and stir in the rest of the butter, simmering until the sauce thickens somewhat.

Cut the twine and remove it. Serve the pheasant drizzled with the brandy sauce.

CELERIAC ROAST WITH CITRUS SAUCE

Serves 4 as a meat-free main course

1 (2-pound/900-g) celeriac

2 to 3 tablespoons butter, softened

1 coffee spoon fennel seeds

1 coffee spoon caraway seeds

Flaky sea salt and freshly ground black pepper

1 head garlic, separated into cloves but unpeeled, plus 1 to 2 heads halved horizontally

2 to 3 oranges, halved

2 to 3 clementines, halved

1 to 2 lemons, halved

FOR THE CITRUS SAUCE

3 tablespoons orange marmalade

Leaves from 1 to 2 sprigs fresh rosemary, finely chopped, plus 1 whole sprig for garnish

2 bay leaves

1 tablespoon coarse mustard

1 tablespoon red wine vinegar

A splash of brandy or whiskey

Sea salt and freshly ground black pepper

Prepare

Thoroughly wash the celeriac; a brush (a clean toothbrush) works well for reaching between the roots. Dry and (using clean hands!) rub with butter all over. Place on top of two sheets of aluminum foil that you have stacked crosswise.

Briefly crush the fennel and caraway using a pestle and mortar. Sprinkle the celeriac with salt, pepper, and the ground seeds. Also top with the (unpeeled) loose garlic cloves. Fold the foil over the celeriac so it is is nicely sealed and place on a baking sheet.

Make

Preheat the oven to 350°F (180°C).

Bake the celeriac for about 2 hours, until you can effortlessly puncture it with a sharp knife. For the last 30 minutes, place the halved oranges, clementines, and lemons as well as the halved garlic bulb on the baking sheet alongside the celeriac in the oven.

Open the foil, remove the loose garlic cloves, and roast the celeriac uncovered for another 30 minutes to get a nice brown crust.

In the meantime—this can be easily done after you serve the starter—quickly make the sauce: Warm up the marmalade along with the chopped rosemary and the bay leaves in a saucepan. Squeeze 2 of the roasted orange halves, 2 of the clementine halves, and perhaps 1 lemon half, all of which should be still warm from the oven, over the mixture. (Naturally, keep some of the roasted fruits for garnish.)

Press some roasted garlic gloves and stir these into the sauce. Stir in the mustard and slowly bring the sauce to a boil. Douse with vinegar and a splash of brandy. Season with some salt and pepper.

Place the celeriac on a large (preheated!) dish. Pour the sauce over it. Arrange the rest of the roasted fruits around the celeriac and garnish with a handsome sprig of rosemary, which will now look suspiciously like a pine twig.

PORK RIB ROAST WITH PRUNE & PEAR SAUCE

Serves 6 to 8

FOR THE SAUCE

16 pitted prunes

3 pears, peeled, quartered, and cored

1 (750-ml) bottle white wine

2 cinnamon sticks

6 tablespoons (75 g) sugar

2 cups (500 ml) chicken stock

Leaves from 5 sprigs fresh thyme, finely chopped, plus some extra sprigs for garnish

1 shallot, minced

Sea salt and freshly ground black pepper

FOR THE MEAT

1 (3- to 3½-pound/1.5-kg) pork rib roast (ask your butcher to clean the ribs; these are basically connected pork chops)

3 tablespoons olive oil

Leaves from about 5 sprigs fresh thyme

2 small cloves garlic, minced

Sea salt and freshly ground black pepper

Prepare

Make the sauce: In a large pan, bring the prunes, pears, wine, cinnamon sticks, and sugar to a boil, then lower the heat. Let simmer for 25 minutes, then strain through a sieve over another pan, reserving the prunes and pears. To the cooking liquid, add the stock, thyme, and shallot.

Bring to a boil again and simmer until the liquid is reduced by about half, 20 to 25 minutes. Season with salt and pepper and let cool. Cover until ready to use. Cover the prunes and pears, let cool, and store everything in the fridge until dinnertime.

Rub the meat with the oil, thyme, and garlic and sprinkle with salt and pepper. Cover and refrigerate until ready to use.

Make

Remove the meat from the fridge so it can reach room temperature. The meat needs to be cooked for about 1¼ to 1½ hours and rest for 15 minutes, so make sure to plan the start of your dinner well.

Preheat the oven to 400°F (200°C).

Place the roast in a baking dish. Roast for about 1¼ to 1½ hours, until nicely pink on the inside (if you happen to have a meat thermometer, the internal temperature should be about 150°F/65°C). Turn the meat halfway through the cooking time.

Cover loosely with aluminum foil and allow the meat to rest on a carving board for 15 minutes.

Meanwhile, heat up the sauce in a saucepan and add the poached prunes and pears.

Place the roast on a (preheated!) serving dish and pour some of the sauce over it. Serve the remaining sauce separately.

CHARRED OXHEART CABBAGE WITH TARRAGON, FISH SAUCE & BROWN BUTTER

Serves 2

1 tablespoon olive oil

½ medium-size oxheart cabbage or white cabbage, outer leaves removed

About 4 tablespoons (55 g) butter, at room temperature

2 to 3 tablespoons Thai fish sauce, or home made garum (page 265)

2 teaspoons apple cider vinegar or white wine vinegar

Sea salt (if needed) and freshly ground black pepper

1 tablespoon fresh tarragon, finely chopped

Heat the oil in a medium cast-iron or other heavy-bottomed skillet over medium heat. Place the halved cabbage cut sides down in the pan. Just leave it to cook for 10 to 15 minutes, until the underside has become beautifully charred.

Lower the heat somewhat, add half of the butter, and shake the pan in order to spread the butter under and all around the cabbage. Once the butter has melted and begins to foam, tilt the pan toward you and spoon the butter over the cabbage, making sure to coat everything. Do this for half a minute, allowing the cabbage to cook further. As soon as the butter starts to brown, add another lump and repeat the process.

Stick a knitting needle or a steel skewer into the heart of the cabbage: Is it done yet? You should be able to pull out the skewer without effort. If not, allow the cabbage to tenderize some more. Douse with the fish sauce. Sprinkle the cabbage with the vinegar and season with salt (if needed) and pepper. Sprinkle with the tarragon and serve.

RUM-CURED & SMOKED WILD SALMON

Serves 4

½ cup (100 g) lightly packed dark
   brown sugar

8 teaspoons (50 g) coarse sea salt

18 ounces (500 g) fresh wild
   salmon fillet, with skin

½ cup (125 ml) brown rum

Freshly ground black pepper

HOW TO QUICKLY MAKE YOUR OWN SMOKER BOX

Even if you don't own a smoker box, this recipe is still easy to make. Line a roasting pan or a baking sheet with aluminum foil. Scatter some smoking chips (available at cookware stores, or in the barbecue section at supermarkets) over the foil. (Tea leaves also work fine, by the way.) Top with a second layer of foil. On top of the foil layers, place a rack that fits your roasting pan. This can be an oven rack, a grate from your microwave, or a stainless-steel pan trivet, as long as it's heatproof.

Put the fish on the grate, place over the stove, turn on the burner, and wait for it to begin smoking. Then turn down the heat and thoroughly cover the roasting pan with a large sheet of aluminum foil. Make sure there are no cracks by pressing the edges to seal them tightly. Of course you wouldn't want the smoke to escape.

Although a fatty fish lends itself best for smoking, really any type of fish can be smoked. Cure the fish (or meat!) beforehand; otherwise the fish can easily turn out bland. This can be done in a brine bath but also by rubbing the fish with salt. Allowing the fish to dry for a couple of hours in the refrigerator before smoking will yield the best results. You can do this on a grate, but the more impatient chef can also get a nice result by simply dabbing with some paper towels.

I like making this dish for large groups. It's relatively fast and an easy way to serve many people. The recipe is for about 18 ounces (500 g) salmon, but feel free to multiply it when (like me) you are preparing a whole side of salmon. You will likely draw some oohs! and aahs! from your guests when you place an entire fish on the table. Begin preparations the evening before your big dinner party. It's not much work, really, but the fish needs to cure overnight.

Prepare

Sprinkle a pinch each of the brown sugar and the salt in the bottom of a shallow baking dish. Place the salmon on top, skin down. Sprinkle with the rum and the rest of the brown sugar and salt. Grind some pepper over it. Let stand at least 6 hours or overnight in the refrigerator.

Remove the salmon from the liquid that will have accumulated and carefully dab the fish with a paper towel. Put it on a rack in the fridge and let dry (this can take a day or a couple of hours) until you are about to sit down for dinner.

Make

Prepare your smoker as described at left and put the fish in place to start smoking. Smoke the salmon for about 15 minutes, until tender. The thickness of your salmon will determine how long it takes for your fish to be done. Smoking a whole side of salmon will take a little longer. By "done," I mean that the top surface of the fish will be pale, or light pink, and the center still nearly raw although no longer ice-cold.

I really like this dish with horseradish mustard (page 259) and lots of green vegetables.

My backyard, Christmas 2016

Marie in the front yard. Christmas 2016

ROASTED CAULIFLOWER WITH GOAT CHEESE CREAM

***Serves 2 as a main dish
or 4 as a side***

FOR THE CAULIFLOWER

1 whole head cauliflower, leaves
   removed

1 (750-ml) bottle white wine

1 teaspoon chile flakes, or to taste

Zest of 1 lemon

2 tablespoons butter

Olive oil

Sea salt and freshly ground black
   pepper

FOR THE GOAT
CHEESE CREAM

7 ounces (200 g) fresh goat cheese

3½ ounces (100 g) cream cheese,
   at room temperature

Freshly ground black pepper

A pinch of chile flakes

Depending on the size of the cauliflower and the amount of side dishes you'll be serving, this makes for a great vegetarian main course for two to four people. For a larger group you can easily serve two or three heads of cauliflower. You can precook them, one at a time, in the same pan and pour in some extra wine and/or water if too much has evaporated.

Prepare

Put the cauliflower, wine, chile flakes, lemon zest, butter, and a splash of water (so the cauliflower is about half submerged) in a large saucepan and cook, covered, until half done, about 15 minutes. Set aside until ready to roast.

Make the goat cheese cream: Puree the goat cheese and cream cheese in a food processor until completely smooth. Grind some black pepper over the mixture. Set aside in the food processor until ready to serve.

Make

Preheat the oven to 400°F (200°C) and grease a baking dish with a splash of oil.

Sprinkle the cauliflower with salt and pepper. Place it in the dish and bake for 30 to 40 minutes, until nicely golden brown. A sharp knife should cut through it without effort.

Process the goat cheese cream again until smooth and spoon a nice layer onto a serving platter. Sprinkle with a pinch of chile flakes. Place the cauliflower on top and serve.

PASTY OF DEER & ALE

Serves about 6

FOR THE STEW

A small handful of all-purpose flour

Sea salt and freshly ground black pepper

2¼ pounds (1 kg) boneless venison shoulder or foreleg, cubed; you can also ask the butcher for venison stew meat

Olive oil

2 large onions, peeled and diced

3 to 5 small cloves garlic, minced

2 carrots, peeled and diced

2 ribs celery, diced

5¼ ounces (150 g) bacon, diced

2 tablespoons mustard

½ tablespoon fennel seeds, crushed in a mortar

½ tablespoon coriander seeds, crushed in a mortar

2½ cups (600 ml) ale (2 bottles) or another strong beer

2 cups (500 ml) game (or beef) stock, plus a little extra

1 tablespoon dark brown sugar

3 tablespoons red wine vinegar

A generous pinch of freshly grated nutmeg

8 juniper berries, crushed

Leaves from 3 sprigs fresh rosemary

FOR ON TOP

½ (17.3-ounce/490-g) box frozen puff pastry dough (1 sheet), thawed

1 egg, beaten

If you want to make a splash while keeping things foolproof, you can prepare a game stew, and to make it even more festive, cover it with a beautiful dough layer decorated with stars and hearts. Stew is easy to make for large parties and if you make it a day in advance, its flavor will only improve. By using game for this recipe you give this humble stew an extra-festive character.

Prepare

Season the flour with salt and pepper and coat the pieces of venison with it. Pat off any excess flour. Heat up a generous splash of oil in a heavy-bottomed pan and brown the meat spread out on the bottom in one single layer. Do this in batches; if the pan is too full, the meat will steam instead of sear.

Scoop the meat from the pan and keep it warm on a plate covered by a lid. Add another splash of oil to the pan and sauté the onions, garlic, carrots, celery, and bacon for a couple of minutes while stirring continuously. Add the seared meat, stir everything, and spoon in the mustard, fennel seeds, and coriander seeds. Douse with the ale. Pour in enough of the stock to submerge everything. Bring to a boil and stir in the brown sugar, vinegar, nutmeg, juniper berries, and rosemary. Turn down the heat and allow the stew to simmer for at least 2 hours, but sometimes even 3 hours over very low heat. The cooking time depends on the quality of the meat and the size of the venison pieces. After 2 hours, check whether the meat has become tender enough; if not, let it simmer some more. If needed, season with salt and pepper.

Deer meat is naturally fairly dry; make sure that there's enough liquid in the pan, and add some more stock if needed. Let the stew cool somewhat, then scoop into a nice large baking dish.

Roll out the puff pastry on a floured countertop. Make a hole in the middle (for the hot steam) using an apple corer or a dough cutter. Brush the rim of the baking dish with some beaten egg and place the sheet of dough on top. Carefully press the edges of the dough onto the dish and trim the excess, leaving a margin of one centimeter all around—dough tends to shrink a little. Decorate the puff pastry lid with the dough trimmings and refrigerate the entire baking dish until ready to bake.

Make

Preheat the oven to 400°F (200°C).

Bake the stew in the oven for 35 to 40 minutes, until the dough has turned golden brown and the stew underneath begins to bubble.

CHRISTMAS PORCHETTA

Serves 8 to 10

1 pork belly (at least
    4½ pounds/2 kg), without rind

Salt and Sichuan or black
    peppercorns, crushed in a
    mortar

3 tablespoons olive oil, plus more
    for the roasting pan

FOR THE FILLING

5 teaspoons coarse sea salt, plus
    some extra

3 tablespoons Sichuan or black
    peppercorns, crushed in a
    mortar

1 large bunch fresh flat-leaf
    parsley (about 1¾ ounces/50 g),
    coarsely chopped

1 bunch thyme, finely chopped

Leaves from 6 sprigs fresh
    rosemary, finely chopped

Grated zest of 2 oranges

Seeds from 6 to 8 cardamom pods,
    crushed in a mortar

6 small cloves garlic, minced

About ½ cup plus 2 tablespoons
    (80 g) hazelnuts, briefly toasted
    in a skillet, coarsely chopped

ALSO NEEDED

Kitchen twine: cut 8 (12-inch/
    30-cm) pieces

Beware: The roast needs to be cooked in the oven for more than 3 hours, so plan accordingly. The result will be quite something, though. Yes, it's very fatty meat, but that's what makes this so delicious. This dish is impossible to ruin; if you leave it in the oven for 30 minutes too long it won't matter. Serve with something fresh-zesty. I like the horseradish mustard on page 259, for example. And the beets found on the same page also go great with this porchetta.

Such a substantial roulade serves a crowd, and whatever you have left over (if you manage to not finish all of it) will still be delicious the day after.

Prepare

Place the meat on a cutting board, skin side facing up. Use a sharp knife to score the fat, making shallow cuts spaced about ⅓ inch (8 mm) apart. Turn the pork belly over. Sprinkle with salt and some Sichuan peppercorn.

Combine all ingredients for the filling and spread it out over the meat. Tightly roll up the meat and carefully tie it together using the pieces of kitchen twine you have ready. Start in the middle, then tie up the ends, then tie twine in the spaces between.

Rub the outside of your roulade with salt and Sichuan peppercorn as well. Refrigerate until ready to roast. You can do this a day early so the meat will marinate even better.

Make

Remove the meat from the fridge at least an hour in advance, allowing it to reach room temperature.

Preheat the oven to 450°F (230°C).

Grease a roasting pan with some oil and put in the roulade. Roast for 20 minutes, lower the temperature to 300°F (150°C), and thoroughly cover the roulade with aluminum foil. Cook for another 2½ hours. Remove the foil and baste the meat with the liquid from the roasting pan. Cook uncovered for about 15 minutes more, until the crust has nicely browned.

Remove the porchetta from the roasting pan and let rest on a carving board for 15 minutes. Sometimes it's pretty stuck so you may have to carefully pry it loose from the pan. Cut into thin slices. Eat warm or cold.

Our traditional Christmas family barbecue

GUINEA FOWL WITH PROSECCO—GREEN GRAPE SAUCE

Serves 4

7 tablespoons (100 g) butter, plus extra for sautéing the onions

Sea salt and freshly ground black pepper

1 (2¼-pound/1-kg) whole guinea fowl

1 cup (250 ml) prosecco or dry white wine, plus a little extra

1 red onion, diced

1 small clove garlic, crushed

4½ ounces (125 g) bacon, diced

1 tablespoon all-purpose flour

1²⁄₃ cups (400 ml) chicken stock

Leaves of 3 sprigs fresh thyme

1 bay leaf

2 handfuls seedless green grapes, halved

Look, roasting a turkey is not that easy. Because of its size, different parts of the bird will cook differently. So after all your effort you'll often end up with a dry turkey breast or undercooked legs. Why don't you go easy on yourself and choose guinea fowl instead? They are a bit smaller than turkey, but if you have a table full of dinner guests you can simply cook two or three birds. The meat is nicely firm, they are easy to prepare, and by adding this succulent and tasty sauce you will make all family members happy. Including yourself.

Mash the butter with salt and pepper to taste. Thoroughly wash your hands. Then, starting at the bird's neck, carefully slide your fingers in between the skin and the breast meat. Do this extremely carefully—take off any rings you may be wearing because the skin shouldn't tear. If all goes well, you will have formed two pockets on either side of the breastbone. Press butter into these pockets and then spread the butter mixture evenly over the entire fowl by rubbing its skin on the outside. Sprinkle the outside with salt and pepper as well. Place in a buttered baking dish and pour a splash of prosecco all around.

Preheat the oven to 350°F (180°C) if you want to continue straightaway; otherwise, cover and store the fowl in the fridge until ready to roast. This can be done a day in advance.

Make the sauce: Melt a lump of butter in a saucepan. Add the onion, garlic, and bacon and fry, stirring, for 3 to 4 minutes, until the onion softens. Stir in the flour and cook everything together for another 2 minutes. Douse with the prosecco. Cook until reduced somewhat, pour in the stock, and add the thyme and bay leaf. If necessary, season with salt and pepper. Simmer for 20 minutes, allowing the sauce to reduce. Two minutes before the end, add the grapes so they can warm up a little. Set aside until ready to serve.

If you prepared and refrigerated the guinea fowl in advance, remove it from the fridge so it can reach room temperature.

Preheat the oven to 350°F (180°C).

Roast the fowl for about 1 hour, until nicely golden brown. During roasting, baste the bird with its cooking liquid twice so it becomes extra juicy and delicious. After removing it from the oven, let the bird rest for 10 minutes, covered by a sheet of aluminum foil.

Slowly bring the sauce to a near boil. Pour half of it over the guinea fowl and serve the rest in a bowl on the side.

VEGETABLE SPIRAL TART WITH AVOCADO-CURRY CREAM

Serves 4 to 6

FOR THE CRUST

About 1 pound (450 g) sweet
　　potatoes, peeled

1 egg

Sea salt and freshly ground black
　　pepper

FOR THE FILLING

3 large carrots (about
　　11 ounces/300 g), peeled

2 parsnips, peeled

1 eggplant

2 eggs

½ cup plus 2 tablespoons (150 ml)
　　heavy cream

1 small clove garlic, pressed or
　　grated

1 teaspoon curry powder

1 teaspoon caraway seeds

ON THE SIDE

1 avocado

1 teaspoon curry powder

Grated zest and juice of ½ lemon

½ cup (125 ml) crème fraîche

Prepare

Preheat the oven to 350°F (180°C).

Cut a piece of parchment paper to size so it fits a 9-inch (22-cm) pie pan. Grease everything, including the parchment paper.

Grate the sweet potatoes in a food processor using a coarse grater. Beat the egg with some salt and pepper and combine it with the sweet potato. Press the sweet potato mixture into the pie pan, forming an even layer on the bottom and up the sides. Prebake the crust on the lower rack in the oven until half done and the edges begin to brown, about 25 minutes. Let cool somewhat on a rack.

Increase the oven temperature to 400°F (200°C).

Meanwhile, make the filling: Shave the vegetables as thinly as you dare into strips. I use a vegetable peeler for the carrots and the parsnips. That works better than you might think. For the eggplant I use a chef's knife to cut very thin slivers.

Whisk the eggs and cream together with the garlic, curry powder, and caraway. Season with salt and pepper.

Fit the vegetables in the pan in circles, artfully alternating among different colors so it will look beautiful. Continue until all have been used up. After filling the whole pan I always stick the final slivers left on the counter in between the vegetable spirals. You can really use everything!

Pour the egg mixture over the vegetables, carefully spreading it out. Bake the tart for at least 45 minutes, until done. Let rest for 10 minutes before removing it from the pan. If you are planning to serve the tart later you should bake it for only 35 minutes. In that case it will go back into the oven just before serving. Let cool, cover, and store in the fridge until ready to serve.

Make the avocado cream: Puree the avocado together with the curry powder and the lemon zest and juice in the food processor until completely smooth. Stir in the crème fraîche. Cover and refrigerate until ready to serve.

Make

Allow the tart to reach room temperature. Preheat the oven to 400°F (200°C). Bake the tart for about 15 minutes, until nicely done and warm throughout. Serve with the cold avocado cream.

CURRY CAULIFLOWER CHRISTMAS PASTY WITH ALMONDS & APRICOTS

Serves 6 to 8

FOR THE FILLING

1 tablespoon olive oil

2 onions, diced

4 ribs celery, finely diced

2 small cloves garlic, minced

1 tablespoon curry powder

1 tablespoon paprika

4 heaping tablespoons (70 g) tomato paste

1 head cauliflower, ground into crumbs in a food processor

½ cup (100 g) red lentils

2 cups (500 ml) vegetable stock

¾ cup (100 g) almonds, finely chopped

¾ cup (100 g) dried apricots, halved

1½ cups (150 g) grated aged cheese

4 eggs, beaten

A generous bunch of fresh flat-leaf parsley, chopped

Sea salt and freshly ground black pepper

FOR THE DOUGH

3½ cups (450 g) all-purpose flour

2 teaspoons salt

¾ cup plus 1 tablespoon (200 ml) milk

7 tablespoons (100 g) butter

1 egg, beaten

ON THE SIDE

1⅔ cups (400 ml) sour cream

Some scallion rings

Sea salt and freshly ground pepper

Optional: fresh garden herbs

This is a beautiful and very tasty vegetarian dish for the Christmas dinner table. If you serve this pasty to avowed carnivores they will believe they're eating meatloaf. Please adjust your choice of herbs to your own taste. In this case I'm opting for the rather neutral-tasting parsley, but throwing in a handful of fresh cilantro will render the dish more Indian and make it a perfect companion for some raita (a yogurt sauce with cucumber and garam masala) instead of the sour cream I use here. So consider this recipe as a starting point.

Note to the chef: Make sure to knead the dough just briefly! Really swiftly, just until it starts to come together. Otherwise it will become compact and stiff. It really is an easy dough, however, one that pretty much always succeeds and bakes nicely—including on the bottom, which for many pie doughs is not a given.

Prepare

Make the filling: In a large heavy-bottomed pan, heat the oil. Sauté the onions and celery until soft. Add the garlic. Cook everything for a while. Add the curry powder, paprika, and tomato paste. While stirring, cook for several minutes, until it starts to smell sweet and spicy. Then stir in the cauliflower crumbs and the lentils. Douse with the stock. Cover and let simmer gently for about 20 minutes. Stir occasionally while reducing it into a thick paste that's no longer wet but doesn't burn and stick to the bottom of the pan either. Remove from the heat and let cool somewhat.

Make the dough

Grease a 9-inch (22-cm) springform pan (or a pie pan) and dust it with flour. Mix the flour and salt. Put the milk and the butter in a saucepan, add ½ cup plus 2 tablespoons (150 ml) water, and heat until the butter has melted.

Add the flour in one batch and thoroughly stir everything into one firm ball. Remove it from the pan and quickly knead it on a floured countertop into a coherent dough. Let the dough rest for a while. Divide the dough into one third and two thirds. Roll out the larger part and use it to line the springform pan, allowing some overhang around the edges.

CONTINUED

Christmas Shopping, Canal Saint-Martin, Paris

Preheat the oven to 350°F (180°C).

Stir the almonds, apricots, and cheese into the cauliflower filling, followed by the beaten eggs and the parsley. Season with salt and pepper.

Spoon the filling into the dough-lined springform pan. Roll out the remaining dough and use it to cover the pasty filling.

Use an apple corer to cut three holes in the top crust. Trim the edges and roll out the trimmings. Cut Christmas decorations from this dough and stick them onto the pasty with some beaten egg. Glaze the entire top of the pasty with the remaining egg.

Bake for 1 hour. Use a skewer to check whether the filling is done: Every oven is different. Sometimes it takes a little longer, sometimes it doesn't. Loosely cover the pasty with aluminum foil if the top is browning too fast.

Serve immediately, while still warm, or let cool and serve cold. You can always reheat the pasty later.

Make

You can heat up the pasty covered with aluminum foil. It will take about 20 minutes in an oven preheated to 350°F (180°C). Serve with sour cream (seasoned with some scallion rings, salt and pepper, and some fresh garden herbs if you want).

169

DUTCH BABY WITH NETTLE CHEESE & STEAMED LEEKS

Makes 1 large or 4 small pancakes; serves 4

FOR THE TOPPING

6 medium leeks (about 5½ pounds/2.5 kg)

1 tablespoon olive oil

1 tablespoon butter

Sea salt and freshly ground black pepper

⅓ cup (75 ml) dry white wine

1 cup (250 ml) vegetable or chicken stock

Leaves of 4 sprigs fresh thyme, plus a little extra for garnish

1⅓ cups (150 g) grated Dutch nettle cheese

FOR THE DUTCH BABY

3 eggs, at room temperature

½ cup plus 2 tablespoons (150 ml) whole milk, preferably also at room temperature

½ cup plus 2 tablelspoons (75 g) all-purpose flour

Grated zest of ½ lemon

A pinch of freshly grated nutmeg

A pinch of sea salt

About 3½ tablespoons (50 g) butter, cubed

Although the Dutch baby is a popular brunch dish in the United States, in the Netherlands it is relatively unknown, even though the recipe was seemingly named after us. But appearances are deceiving: This is actually a German dish, a twist on the *Pfannkuchen*. The Pennsylvania Dutch, a German-speaking immigrant community in the United States, made them, so technically they should be called "Deutsch" babies.

Prepare

Preheat the oven to 400°F (200°C).

Remove the dark green part and the tough outer layers of the leeks but leave the root ends intact so they won't fall apart. Halve the stalks lengthwise if they are medium sized; leave the thin ones intact. Thoroughly wash them to remove any sand between the layers! Pat dry.

Heat the oil and butter in a large deep oval ovenproof skillet over medium heat. Place the leeks in the pan, season with salt and pepper, and slowly cook them for about 5 minutes, turning them occasionally. Make sure they stay intact as much as possible. Pour in the wine, let evaporate almost completely, then pour in the stock. Place the thyme on top.

Cover the pan and transfer to the oven to slowly tenderize for about 20 minutes. Scoop the leeks from the pan and let cool until ready to use.

Make

Place a large ovenproof skillet (or four small skillets) on the middle rack of the oven and preheat to 430°F (225°C).

Beat the eggs until pale and foamy using a hand mixer at high speed. Use a whisk to mix in the milk, flour, lemon zest, nutmeg, and salt and continue beating by hand to make a smooth and thin batter.

Open the oven and slide a lump of butter into the skillet(s). It will melt immediately, so tilt the pan back and forth (wear oven mitts!) to evenly spread the butter. Pour the batter into the scorching-hot pan(s) straight away, quickly put in the leeks, sprinkle with the cheese, and close the oven. Bake the pancake(s) until inflated and done, about 20 minutes.

Serve on a large plate and sprinkle with some fresh thyme. The Dutch baby will deflate a bit, but that is normal.

SIDE DISHES

STUFFED BAKED APPLES

Serves 4

1 (750-ml) bottle apple cider

2 tablespoons butter

4 large apples (Fuji)

About ⅔ cup (150 g) mincemeat
(page 261)

¾ cup (75 g) walnuts, coarsely
chopped

1 tablespoon chopped stem ginger
in syrup

These apples are terrifically delicious with ice cream, unsweetened crème fraîche, or cold custard (page 255), but I place them with the side dishes, as they work so well in a hearty meal: Serve them with sauerkraut and the pheasant of page 142. Isn't it fun?

Prepare

Cook the apple cider and butter in a saucepan until reduced to one third the mixture's original volume. Cover and set aside until ready to bake.

Core the apples with an apple corer. Do this generously, making a wide opening so that you can really fill them. Mix the mincemeat with the walnuts. Fill the cavities of the apples with the mixture. Position them in a baking dish and cover until ready to bake. (Refrigerate them if they need to stand for a while).

Make

Let the apples come to room temperature and pour the reduced cider around them.

Preheat the oven to 350°F (180°C).

Slide the apples into the oven and bake them for 25 minutes until they release some liquid and are nicely tender. Spoon the cider over the apples once or twice while they're baking to prevent them from drying out. Serve warm.

MASHED POTATOES WITH CELERIAC & APPLE

Serves 4 to 6

18 ounces (500 g) celeriac, peeled and cubed

18 ounces (500 g) mealy potatoes, peeled and cubed

2 apples (Cortland or Braeburn), peeled and cubed

Sea salt and freshly ground black pepper

A pinch of freshly grated nutmeg

3 tablespoons butter

1 tablespoon minced fresh flat-leaf parsley, plus some extra for garnish

2 tablespoons dry breadcrumbs

Terribly easy, as you can make this recipe in advance, and before serving the first course you just pop it into the oven. By adding apple and celeriac, the mashed potatoes become a wonderful companion for game (see page 163) or a stew, like the one on page 156.

Prepare

Bring a pan of water to a boil. Add some salt once the water boils and then the celeriac, and after 15 minutes add the potatoes and apples. Cook for another 20 minutes, until everything is tender. Drain well (celeriac especially contains a lot of liquid). Mash everything; I like to first mash the celeriac so that I can drain the liquid some more, and then I proceed with the rest. You can also use a potato ricer.

Season the puree with salt, pepper, and nutmeg. Fold in the butter and parsley and serve, or if you wish to serve it later, let the puree cool completely and keep in the fridge. Use an ice cream scoop to form balls and place them in a buttered oven dish. Cover until ready to reheat.

Make

Preheat the oven to 350°F (180°C).

Sprinkle the potato balls with the breadcrumbs mixed with parsley, salt, and pepper. Bake them for about 20 minutes, until golden brown.

CARROT TATIN WITH GOAT CHEESE

Serves 4 to 6

18 ounces (500 g) carrots in a mix of colors, peeled

1 thumb-size piece fresh ginger, sliced

2 lemon slices

Sea salt

A splash of olive oil

A cube of butter

½ cup (75 g) grated Dutch goat cheese

½ (17.3-ounce/490-g) box frozen puff pastry dough (1 sheet), thawed

Prepare

Cook the carrots for a few minutes in boiling water with the ginger and lemon slices and a spoonful of salt until they are nearly al dente. Drain and sprinkle with oil.

Butter an 8 x 8-inch (20 x 20-cm) square baking dish, line with parchment paper, and butter the paper. Place the carrots in a single layer in the dish. Sprinkle with the cheese.

Roll out the puff pastry on a floured countertop until you have a sheet that fits over the carrots. Make a hole in the middle with an apple corer, to allow steam to escape. Place the dough on top of the carrots and tuck in the edges. Refrigerate until ready to bake.

Make

Preheat the oven to 400°F (200°C).

Bake the carrot tatin for 15 to 20 minutes, until golden brown, let rest for 2 minutes, then invert the baking dish onto a plate and serve immediately.

CELERY ALMOND SALAD

Serves 4 to 6

3 tablespoons olive oil

2 tablespoons fresh lemon juice

4 tablespoons (25 g) grated Parmesan cheese

1 15-ounce (425-g) can white cannellini beans, drained and rinsed

8 large ribs celery, peeled and very thinly shaved

3 tablespoons raisins, ideally sultanas (golden raisins)

½ cup (75 g) halved almonds, briefly toasted in a dry skillet

Sea salt and freshly ground black pepper

5¼ ounces (150 g) arugula

1 handful chopped fresh garden herbs, such as parsley, dill, basil, and chives

Prepare

Whisk the oil, lemon juice, and cheese in a bowl, and stir in the cannellini beans. Scoop in the celery, raisins, and nearly all the almonds, keeping some almonds aside for garnish. Season if you wish with salt and pepper.

Let stand for 15 minutes to allow the flavors to be absorbed.

Make

Before serving, toss the arugula and the herbs through the salad, and serve immediately.

My Amsterdam kitchen

BROCCOLI POT PIES

Serves 4

¾ cup plus 1 tablespoon (200 ml)
crème fraîche

⅔ cup (100 g) Dutch goat cheese,
grated

1 to 2 teaspoons plus 2 tablespoons
caraway seeds, briefly toasted in
a dry skillet

4 scallions, sliced

1 substantial head broccoli, cut into
small florets

¾ cup (100 g) frozen shelled peas
and/or cooked shelled fava beans

1 egg, beaten

½ (17.3-ounce/490-g) box frozen
puff pastry dough (1 sheet),
thawed and cut into four squares

In a large bowl, mix the crème fraîche, cheese, 1 to 2 teaspoons caraway, the scallions, broccoli, and peas and divide among four small ovenproof baking dishes. Wet the rims of the bowls with a bit of egg and place the dough sheets on top. Cut and fold them so they fit or let them hang loose. Brush with egg and sprinkle with the 2 tablespoons caraway seeds. Keep in the fridge until ready to bake.

Make

Preheat the oven to 400°F (200°C).

Bake for 25 to 30 minutes, until the crust is golden brown and crispy.

MUSTARD GRATIN WITH POTATOES & PARSNIPS

Serves 6 to 8

Sea salt

1⅔ pounds (750 g) waxy potatoes, cut into ½-inch (1.5-cm) cubes

1⅔ pounds (750 g) parsnips, cut into ½-inch (1.5-cm) cubes

5 tablespoons (75 g) butter

½ cup plus 2 tablespoons (75 g) all-purpose flour

About 2½ cups (600 ml) milk

2 tablespoons coarse mustard

2 tablespoons white wine vinegar

2 teaspoons fresh thyme leaves

Freshly ground black pepper

A handful of breadcrumbs

About ¼ cup (25 g) grated Parmesan cheese

Prepare

Bring a large saucepan of salted water to a boil. Add the potatoes and parsnips and cook for about 12 minutes, until they are al dente. Drain in a sieve and let the liquid evaporate. Slide them into a baking dish.

Melt the butter in a saucepan, stir in the flour, and cook for about 3 minutes. Stir in the milk and keep stirring—with a whisk—until you have a smooth sauce. Don't worry if your sauce has lumps at first, keep stirring: It will smooth out.

While stirring, allow the sauce to reduce until it has the consistency of thin yogurt. Season with the mustard, vinegar, thyme, salt and pepper. Pour the sauce over the vegetable cubes in the baking dish.

Mix the breadcrumbs with the cheese and some pepper. Sprinkle the entire dish with it. You can do all of this in advance.

Make

Preheat the oven to 350°F (180°C).

Bake the gratin for about 35 minutes, until the top is a nice golden brown and the sauce bubbles beautifully.

BRUSSELS SPROUTS À LA CARBONARA

Serves 6 to 8

Sea salt

2¼ pounds (1 kg) Brussels sprouts, cleaned and halved

5¼ ounces (150 g) bacon, diced

2 small cloves garlic, minced

1 cup (250 ml) heavy cream

½ cup (50 g) grated Parmesan cheese

Freshly ground black pepper

1 small bunch fresh parsley, chopped

I know, I know . . . ! There is no cream in a real carbonara.

But let me put it this way: This dish really does resemble a carbonara, and with cream in it you can easily make it in advance and you'll only have to reheat it before you serve dinner. We're aiming for ease, and foolproof methods. Christmas cooking should remain fun.

Prepare

Bring a large saucepan of salted water to a boil. Add the Brussels sprouts and cook them for 10 minutes. Drain, rinse with cold water, and let stand to drain.

Fry the bacon in a skillet. Add the garlic at the last moment and fry for 2 minutes. Combine with the Brussels sprouts.

Mix the cream and cheese and season with pepper. Set everything aside until ready to serve.

Make

Heat the cream mixture in a skillet. Stir in the Brussels sprouts mixture and cook to heat through. Sprinkle with the parsley and serve.

FULL-FLAVORED RED CABBAGE WITH PEARS & HAZELNUTS

Serves 8

2 tablespoons olive oil

2 onions, sliced

2 small cloves garlic, minced

Leaves of 4 sprigs fresh rosemary, coarsely chopped, plus some extra for garnish

About 15 juniper berries, crushed

½ head red cabbage (about 2¼ pounds/1 kg), cored and sliced

1 teaspoon ground cinnamon

3 tablespoons raw cane sugar

4 tablespoons (60 ml) red wine vinegar

1⅔ cups (400 ml) vegetable stock

2 pears, peeled, cored, and cubed

Sea salt and freshly ground black pepper

Heaping ⅓ cup (50 g) hazelnuts, briefly toasted in a dry skillet

6 tablespoons hazelnut oil

This is a good recipe for red cabbage, I find; I always receive compliments on it. What makes it easy is that it can be served either warm or cold. Serving it cold actually makes things really simple for a Christmas meal.

Prepare

Heat the olive oil in a heavy-bottomed pan. Add the onions and sauté them for about 10 minutes, until soft. Stir in the garlic, rosemary, and juniper berries and sauté them for a minute. Add as much cabbage as will fit in the pan and cook while stirring until it wilts. Then add more cabbage.

Add the cinnamon, sugar, and vinegar, cook for a while, then douse with the stock. Cover the pan and let simmer over low heat for about 45 minutes.

Add the pear cubes about 15 minutes before the end of the cooking time. Season with salt and pepper. Let cool.

Make

Heat up the cabbage in the same pan, stirring continuously, or just leave it at room temperature. Garnish with some extra rosemary leaves and the hazelnuts, and drizzle with a splash of hazelnut oil.

WARM BEAN SALAD WITH CASHEW & KALE PESTO

Serves 6

FOR THE PESTO

½ cup (60 g) unsalted cashews or hazelnuts, toasted, plus some extra for garnish

½ cup (60 g) coarsely grated Parmesan cheese

2 small cloves garlic, pressed

About ⅓ cup (75 ml) grapeseed oil or light olive oil

2¾ ounces (75 g) baby kale

Juice of 1 lemon

FOR THE SALAD

Sea salt

Scant 1 cup (150 g) frozen cooked shelled fava beans

4 cups (250 g) sugar snaps and/or snow peas

4 cups (250 g) haricots verts or green beans

Grated zest of 1 lemon

This is an easy side dish for serving a lot of people. I use haricots verts, sugar snaps, and fava beans (frozen, just as good as fresh), but you can of course choose peas, snow peas, edamame, flageolets (precooked), or what have you. It's the mix of green beans that lends it such a rich flavor.

Prepare

Make the pesto: Combine all the ingredients in a food processor and pulse to puree.

Make the salad: Bring a saucepan of water to a boil. Throw in some salt. Blanch the vegetables one kind at a time, each very briefly: less than 4 minutes! The haricots verts maybe a little longer but the rest really short. Rinse them immediately under cold water, to stop the cooking process.

Scoop in a few spoonfuls of the pesto and immediately transfer the salad to a bowl to serve. Sprinkle with some grated zest and finely chopped nuts.

TIP: You will likely have some leftover pesto, as it's hard to only make a few spoonfuls of pesto. As long as you preserve it under a layer of olive oil in the fridge, you can enjoy it for another 2 weeks or so. Use it the way you would use a pesto Genovese: with pasta, streaked through bread dough (nice with my pumpkin, feta & sage bread on page 35), or on a slice of bread with goat cheese and tomatoes.

OVEN-ROASTED BEETS STUFFED WITH GOAT CHEESE, DATES & CELERY

Serves 4 (one beet per person) or 8 if halved

4 large round beets, cooked and peeled

6 tablespoons (90 ml) olive oil

4 ribs celery, diced

1 small clove garlic, minced

8 dates, pitted and sliced

⅔ cup (75 g) crumbled goat cheese

3 tablespoons balsamic vinegar

1 tablespoon liquid honey

Sea salt and freshly ground black pepper

2 tablespoons pine nuts, briefly toasted in a dry skillet

Serves very well as a starter, by the way. Delicious, really.

Prepare

Slice off the top of each beet and scoop out the center with a sharp little spoon (or a melon baller), to ⅜ inch (1 cm) from the edge. Chop the scooped-out beet.

Heat the oil in a wok or a skillet. Sauté the celery, add the chopped beets and the garlic, and sauté everything. Add the dates. Toss everything around a few times. Take the pan off the heat and mix in the goat cheese. Drizzle in the vinegar, honey, and if you wish some oil, and season everything with salt and pepper.

Put the hollowed-out beets in a baking dish and fill them generously with the goat cheese mixture. Sprinkle with the pine nuts. Cover and refrigerate until ready to bake.

Make

Preheat the oven to 345°F (175°C).

Bake the beets for 20 minutes or more (if you just took them out of the fridge, I'd do 30 minutes), until they are warm through and through and the top is roasted golden brown.

Serve the beets as a starter with an arugula salad on the side, or as a side dish with a nice roasted piece of poultry.

KOHLRABI GRATIN WITH CARAWAY & FETA

Serves 6

2¼ pounds (1 kg) kohlrabi, peeled

2 tablespoons butter

4 small cloves garlic, sliced

1 tablespoon fresh thyme leaves, chopped

A pinch of hot paprika

1 tablespoon caraway seeds

Sea salt and freshly ground black pepper

2 eggs

1 cup (250 ml) heavy cream

1⅓ cups (200 g) crumbled feta cheese

Prepare

Thinly slice the kohlrabi by hand or with a food processor.

Heat the butter in a large, heavy skillet over medium heat, add the kohlrabi, garlic, thyme, paprika, and caraway, and fry for 10 minutes, or until the kohlrabi is tender. Season with salt and pepper.

Butter a baking dish. In a bowl, beat the eggs with the cream and add two-thirds of the crumbled cheese.

Add the kohlrabi mixture from the pan and stir well. Scoop into the prepared baking dish and spread the kohlrabi out evenly. Sprinkle with the remaining feta.

This can go straight into the oven, or you can prepare it a few hours in advance. In that case, refrigerate until ready to bake.

Make

Preheat the oven to 350°F (180°C). Allow the gratin to come to room temperature; this takes about 30 minutes.

Bake the gratin for about 40 minutes.

NEW POTATOES IN JACKETS

Serves 4

18 ounces (500 g) new potatoes

2 egg whites

About 1½ cups (150 g) (home made!) dry breadcrumbs

Sea salt and freshly ground black pepper

1½ teaspoons smoked paprika

½ cup (50 g) finely grated Parmesan cheese

Vegetable oil for deep-frying

Prepare

In a pot of boiling water, cook the potatoes until nearly tender, about 14 minutes, then drain, return to the pot, and let the potatoes cool and the remaining liquid evaporate.

Beat the egg whites in a bowl until foamy. In another bowl, mix the breadcrumbs with salt and pepper to taste, the paprika, and the cheese.

Coat the potatoes in egg whites and then in the breadcrumb mixture. Coat again in the egg whites and the breadcrumb mixture. Keep in the fridge until ready to fry.

Make

In a heavy pot, heat 2 inches (5 cm) oil to 350°F (180°C).

Deep-fry the potatoes in batches until they are golden brown and heated through, 3 to 5 minutes, depending on their size. Let them drain on paper towels.

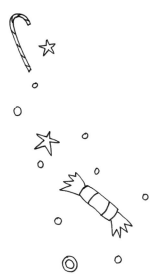

APPLE, WALNUT, CRANBERRY & BROWN RICE SALAD

Serves 4

FOR THE DRESSING

2 small cloves garlic, pressed

1 tablespoon honey

1 teaspoon mustard

2 tablespoons olive oil

2 tablespoons white balsamic or white wine vinegar

Sea salt and freshly ground black pepper to taste

FOR THE SALAD

A few drops of fresh lemon juice

2 apples (Cortland or Braeburn), not peeled, diced

1½ cups (200 g) brown rice, cooked, at room temperature

Heaping ½ cup (75 g) dried cranberries (or raisins), coarsely chopped

1 bunch fresh chives, finely chopped

¾ cup (75 g) walnuts, coarsely chopped

¼ cup (30 g) toasted black sesame seeds

A really delicious side dish that I will easily eat for lunch, too. If you do want to eat it hot, heat up the rice before mixing it. But I like it just warm or at room temperature as well.

If you make the salad at least an hour in advance, the rice can really absorb the flavors, which only improves the dish.

Prepare

Whisk together all the ingredients for the dressing.

Drizzle lemon juice over the apples to prevent discoloration and combine them with the rice, along with the cranberries and chives. Pour the dressing over the salad and toss well. Let the salad stand for a while, to allow the flavors to be absorbed.

Make

Add the walnuts and sesame seeds at the last moment, folding them through the salad, and serve immediately.

Marie in Amsterdam

Family visit at Temple House, County Sligo, Ireland

DESSERTS

TRIFLE WITH SALTY CARAMEL, CHEESECAKE CREAM & CHEWY BROWNIES

Serves 6

FOR THE SALTY CARAMEL SAUCE

1 cup plus 2 tablespoons (225 g) sugar

7 tablespoons (100 g) butter, cubed

½ cup (125 ml) heavy cream

½ teaspoon sea salt

FOR THE BROWNIES

9 tablespoons (125 g) butter, cubed

21 ounces (600 g) dark chocolate (70% cacao or more), in chunks

1⅓ cups (300 g) packed dark brown sugar

8 eggs

4 teaspoons vanilla extract

3 cups plus 2 tablespoons (400 g) all-purpose flour

1 teaspoon sea salt

FOR THE CHEESECAKE CREAM

1 pound (500 g) cream cheese, at room temperature

Seeds of 2 vanilla beans

8 ounces (250 g) mascarpone

1 cup (250 ml) heavy cream

FOR THE CHOCOLATE SAUCE

½ cup plus 2 tablespoons (150 ml) heavy cream

7 ounces (200 g) dark chocolate (70% cacao or more), in chunks

Optional: ¼ cup (60 ml) coffee liqueur or cognac

FOR DECORATING

Nuts, cocoa powder, sparklers, and so on

Make the salty caramel sauce: In a heavy 2-quart saucepan, combine the sugar and ¼ cup (60 ml) water. Place over medium heat and cook, stirring occasionally with a long-handled wooden spoon or heatproof spatula, until the sugar syrup is a medium amber color. Remove from the heat and stir in the butter, one piece at a time. Carefully add the cream (it will bubble up and sputter) and salt. Return to low heat and cook, stirring, until smooth. Set aside to cool to room temperature.

Make the brownies: Preheat the oven to 350°F (180°C). Grease an 8 by 12-inch (20 by 30-cm) or similar-volume baking pan and line the bottom with parchment paper.

Heat the butter, chocolate, and brown sugar in a double boiler until melted and combined. Set aside to cool.

Beat the eggs and vanilla. Stir in the cooled chocolate mixture. In a separate bowl, using a whisk, mix the flour and salt, then combine it with the chocolate mixture with a spatula. Pour the batter into the prepared pan and bake for 25 to 35 minutes, until a skewer inserted in the center comes out with damp crumbs attached (but not wet batter). They should be somewhat soft and fudgy, not too dry! Let cool on a rack.

Make the cheesecake cream: Using a food processor or a hand mixer, combine the cream cheese and the vanilla seeds until smooth and frothy. With the food processor or mixer running, add ¾ cup (200 g) of the cooled caramel sauce and then the mascarpone and cream. Process or beat until soft peaks form. Set aside.

Make the chocolate sauce: Heat the cream over low heat to a near boil. Remove from the heat and add the chocolate, and if you want a splash of coffee liqueur. Allow the warmth of the cream to melt the chocolate; after a couple of minutes, stir to make a smooth sauce.

Assemble the trifle: Starting with the brownie, break it into pieces and form a bottom layer in a large trifle bowl. Drizzle with some of the caramel sauce and spoon some cheesecake cream on top, then drizzle with chocolate sauce. Continue layering until you've used up everything. Cover and refrigerate until ready to serve.

Decorate according to preference: with nuts, cocoa powder, or sparklers. I leave this final touch all up to you.

LIGHT BROWN PAVLOVA WITH POACHED PEARS & CHOCOLATE

Serves 8

FOR THE PAVLOVA

5 egg whites

1 tablespoon cornstarch

1 tablespoon vinegar

A pinch of sea salt

1 cup (125 g) confectioners' sugar

⅔ cup (150 g) firmly packed dark brown sugar

FOR THE POACHED PEARS

1½ pounds (700 g) small pears such as St. Remys or Gieser Wildemans

½ cup (100 g) raw cane sugar

1 (750-ml) bottle moscato d'Asti or another light dessert wine

8 cardamom pods

3 star anise

1 tablespoon pink peppercorns (optional; you don't have to scour the land to find some)

FOR SERVING

½ cup (125 ml) heavy cream, whipped

1¼ cups (300 ml) sour cream

A splash of coffee liqueur or brandy (optional)

3¼ ounces (90 g) dark chocolate, melted in a double boiler (optional)

Confectioners' sugar (optional)

Really everybody likes pavlova, which makes it an excellent dessert for your Christmas dinner. Just do not open the oven while baking. Peek through the window instead. Also, a pavlova will crack—they are supposed to look that way, so basically they can't fail. You can make this a day in advance. If you do, don't store it in the fridge but leave it in the oven until serving. Foam doesn't like condensed moisture. If your pavlova does collapse after all, do not despair: Simply turn it into a trifle using the recipe on the next page. You see, every problem has its solution; *never* panic.

Make the pavlova: Preheat the oven to 400°F (200°C). Line a baking sheet with parchment paper.

In a squeaky-clean bowl, beat the egg whites until soft peaks form. Continue beating while adding the cornstarch, vinegar, and salt.

Mix the sugars together. Once the egg whites form stiff peaks, add the sugar one spoonful at a time, beating constantly and waiting to add the next spoonful until the previous one has been completely absorbed. Continue beating the egg white mixture until stiff and shiny.

Scoop onto the parchment paper–lined baking sheet with a spatula, forming a large circle. Be generous, and shape beautiful curls around the edges with the back of a spoon.

Bake the pavlova for 10 minutes. Lower the oven temperature to 210°F (100°C) and bake for 1 hour longer. Turn off the oven and let the pavlova dry inside the oven for at least 2 hours.

Make the poached pears: Peel the pears, leaving the stems. Place them upright in a large saucepan and add all the other ingredients. If needed, add water so they are well submerged. Cover with parchment paper cut to size and let simmer for about 1 hour, or until they are tender through and through. Using a slotted spoon, gently remove them from their cooking liquid and let cool. Over high heat, boil the cooking liquid until reduced to a syrup. Strain through a sieve and let cool.

To assemble: fold the whipped cream into the sour cream. You can stir in a splash of liqueur, if you'd like. Fill the pavlova with the cream mixture. Arrange the pears on top, and perhaps drizzle some lines of melted chocolate across or sprinkle with powdered sugar. Serve the reduced wine syrup on the side.

PAVLOVA TRIFLE WITH POACHED PEARS

Serves at least 12

Pavlova (see page 212)

Poached pears (see page 212), red
    fruits, or bananas

**FOR THE CARAMEL LAYER
(OPTIONAL)**

2 cups (450 g) packed light brown
    sugar

½ teaspoon salt

½ cup plus 1 tablespoon (125 g)
    butter

2 cups (500 ml) heavy cream

2 tablespoons dark coffee liqueur,
    rum, or cognac (optional)

FOR THE CREAM LAYER

½ cup (125 ml) heavy cream

9 ounces (250 g) mascarpone

2 tablespoons confectioners' sugar

Seeds of 1 vanilla bean

A splash of coffee liqueur or cognac
    (optional)

So, naturally I assume that in your kitchen nothing ever fails. But if, for some reason, it does happen—say you're baking a pavlova and in the midst of a long list of oven dishes to prepare, somehow stress causes you to open the oven door precisely while baking this delicate one—this recipe serves as a First Aid Manual.

Simply turn your pavlova into a trifle; no one will know the difference. On the contrary: Your guests will thank you and think this had been your intention all along. You can set everything in place in advance. After the main course you can put together the trifle in a heartbeat. Yes, I'll say it again: Put it together at the very last moment—the foam in the cream, the caramel, and the pear syrup will dissolve after a while and you wouldn't want two failures in one evening, now, would you?

Prepare

Make the pavlova and the poached pears as described on the previous page and set aside. Store the pavlova in an airtight container, but never in the fridge.

Make the caramel sauce, if you'd like: In a heavy-bottomed pan, over medium heat, stir the brown sugar and salt with the butter until the butter has melted (the mixture will be somewhat grainy). Add the cream and bring the sauce to a boil. While stirring, continue boiling gently until the mixture starts sticking to the back of a spoon. Allow the sauce to cool somewhat and then, if you want, stir in the alcohol.

For the cream layer, whip the heavy cream together with the mascarpone until stiff. Stir in the confectioners' sugar and the vanilla seeds and add a splash of your preferred liqueur to taste if you want. Refrigerate until ready to serve.

Make

In wide dessert glasses, layer pieces of pavlova, cream, and caramel sauce. Finish with the whole pears and pour the reduced pear syrup over each. Serve right away.

VALENÇAY

COEUR DE CHÈVRE

WITTE VAN ROTSELAERE

AGED RIJEN

ETOILE DU BERGER

STE. MAURE

CHEESE PLATTER WITH HOME MADE FRUIT SALAMI

Makes 1 salami (about 12 slices)

FOR THE FRUIT SALAMI

Heaping 1 cup (175 g) dried figs, stems removed and coarsely chopped

¼ teaspoon ground cinnamon

1 teaspoon vanilla extract

A pinch of sea salt

Grated zest of ½ orange or 1 clementine

½ cup (75 g) packed pitted dates, finely chopped

½ cup (75 g) packed dried apricots, finely chopped

½ cup (50 g) pecans, briefly toasted and finely chopped

Sometimes a cheese platter is the only dessert I can eat after a hearty dinner. There are many ways in which to assemble one. You can make a theme-country selection or you can follow the classic method: pick a collection of cheeses ranging from soft to sharp, alternating between white mold cheeses, washed rind, blue cheese, and firm aged cheese, for example. This will also be the order in which to eat them at dinner: You start out with the lighter cheeses and finish with the more piquant types.

Remove all cheeses from the fridge half an hour before serving; that way the flavor of especially the softer cheeses will open up. If you want, you can serve them with a cracker or some good bread, but don't make actual sandwiches. Just eat some bread along with, or after a bite of cheese in order to neutralize the flavor a bit. Cheese without bread works as well, though.

Don't overdo it with the cheese; it really spoils the appetite. A taste is all that matters. I count on serving about 1 tablespoon of each cheese per person and serve three to at most five different types. Often the cheeses will be followed by a sweet dessert (never before), and I don't want my guests to explode.

Serve the platter with slices of home made fruit salami.

Prepare

Make the fruit salami: In a food processor, pulse the figs, cinnamon, vanilla, pinch of salt, and orange zest to a sticky paste. Spoon into a large bowl and combine with the chopped dates, apricots, and pecans and stir to make a smooth and even paste. This is quite a tough task.

Using wet hands to prevent sticking, roll the mixture into a sausage. Cut a large sheet of parchment paper to size and place it on top of a sushi rolling mat. (If you don't have one, you can also do it without.) Place the sausage at the bottom end of the mat and proceed to roll it up in the paper as tightly as possible. Twist the ends of the paper as you would for a toffee and thoroughly tighten so you have a tight sausage in front of you. Store it in the fridge so the sausage can stiffen for at least 2 hours.

Make

Cut the fruit salami into thin slices using a sharp, non-serrated knife and serve alongside the cheese platter. Store leftovers in the fridge.

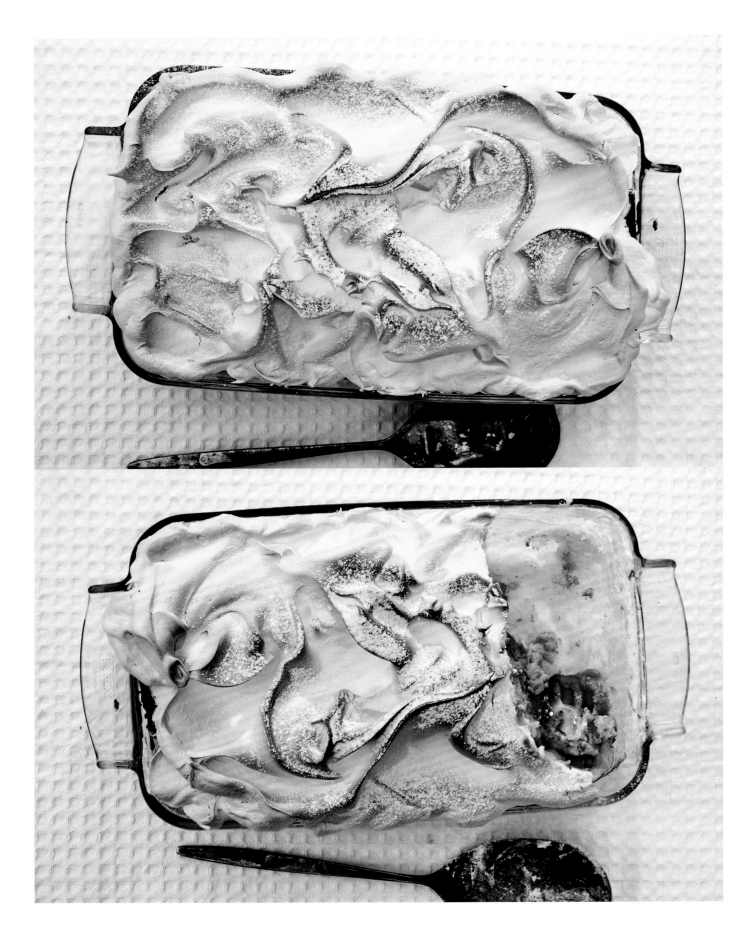

WARM CUSTARD PUDDING WITH BANANA, BELGIAN WAFFLES & MERINGUE

Serves 6

4 eggs

2 cups (500 ml) whole milk

1 vanilla bean, sliced open lengthwise and seeds scraped out

1 cup (200 g) sugar

3 tablespoons all-purpose flour

Sea salt

1 package (about 9 ounces/250 g) Belgian waffles (or home made ones, of course!)

4 ripe bananas, sliced

Confectioners' sugar for serving

Prepare

Separate 3 of the eggs. Add the remaining whole egg to the 3 yolks.

Heat the milk and the scraped vanilla bean and seeds to a simmer, then remove from the heat and allow to steep for 15 minutes.

In a bowl, combine half of the sugar, the flour, and a pinch of salt. Stir in the egg yolks and egg. Remove the bean from the vanilla milk and pour the hot milk into the egg-sugar mixture.

Then pour everything back into the pan and continue stirring until the custard starts to bind nicely. Remove from the heat and let cool somewhat.

Pour a little bit of the custard into a baking dish. Cut the waffles into quarters. Shingle them on top of the custard. Arrange the banana slices in between. Pour the rest of the custard over everything. Cover and refrigerate until ready to bake.

Make

Remove the pudding from the fridge so it can warm to room temperature. Do this well in advance, at least 1 hour.

Preheat the oven to 350°F (180°C). Place the pudding in the oven. Bake for 20 minutes. In the meantime, began preparing the main course (and set a timer).

Whisk the egg whites with a pinch of salt until stiff. Whisk in the remaining sugar in batches until you get a nice, firm meringue. Spread it over the banana pudding, forming beautiful large swirls with a spatula. Place the pudding back in the oven and bake until the meringue begins to brown nicely, 5 to 7 minutes. Keep an eye on it, as this dish can easily burn.

Serve pretty much immediately, sprinkled with confectioners' sugar.

MINCEMEAT FUDGE

Serves 10 to 12

1 (12-ounce/354-ml) can
    evaporated milk

3 tablespoons butter

14 ounces (400 g) dark chocolate
    (70% or higher), coarsely
    chopped

Heaping ½ cup (125 g) mincemeat
    (page 261)

1½ cups (200 g) almonds, briefly
    toasted in a dry skillet and
    chopped

Once you've made mincemeat, this fudge will be . . . a piece of cake. Especially when you serve a cheese platter instead of a sweet dessert, this fudge will work as a nice sweet mini dessert to have with the after-dinner coffee.

While stirring, bring the evaporated milk and the butter to a boil in a saucepan. Remove from the heat and stir in the chocolate, mincemeat, and three-quarters of the almonds. Allow the chocolate to melt completely, stirring occasionally.

Line a 6 by 8-inch (15 by 20-cm) baking pan with parchment paper, with overhang around the edges. Pour in the chocolate mixture and smooth the surface with the back of a wet spoon. Press the remainder of the almonds across the top of the fudge and allow it to stiffen in the fridge for 4 hours.

Use a sharp, non-serrated knife to cut the fudge into small cubes and serve with coffee or put the cubes in a chic little bag so you can offer them to your guests as a sweet present.

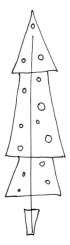

BLOOD ORANGE—MERINGUE TARTLETS

Makes 1 large 9-inch (23-cm) tart or a bunch of individual tartlets (I like these better; you can easily make the pie crusts in a muffin pan—it'll make about 12)

FOR THE CRUST

2⅓ cups (300 g) all-purpose flour

10½ tablespoons (150 g) cold butter, cubed

2 tablespoons sugar

A pinch of sea salt

4 to 6 tablespoons ice-cold water

FOR THE BLOOD ORANGE CURD

½ cup (125 ml) blood orange juice

Juice of 1 lemon

6 egg yolks

3 tablespoons cornstarch

¾ cup (150 g) sugar

10½ tablespoons (150 g) cold butter, cubed

FOR THE MERINGUE

3 egg whites

1 cup plus 2 tablespoons (225 g) sugar

A pinch of sea salt

Prepare

First make the crust: Very briefly pulse the flour, butter, sugar, and salt in a food processor. Add enough cold water for the dough to start coming together. Swiftly shape into a ball, wrap in plastic wrap, and let the dough rest in the fridge for 1 hour.

Preheat the oven to 350°F (180°C). Grease the baking pan or a 12-cup muffin tin with butter.

Roll out the dough to less than ⅛ inch (3 mm) thick on a floured countertop and then use it to line your baking pan(s). Neatly trim the edges. Line each crust with a sheet of parchment paper and fill with pie weights or dried beans. Blind bake a large crust for 20 to 25 minutes, until cooked through and dry; bake small crusts for about 15 minutes. Remove the weights and parchment and return the crusts to the oven for another 8 to 10 minutes, until the crust is golden brown but the edges haven't browned too much. Let the crust(s) cool on a rack.

Make the blood orange curd: Combine the blood orange juice, lemon juice, egg yolks, cornstarch, and sugar in a saucepan. While stirring, bring to a gentle boil and continue stirring until all of the sugar has dissolved and the mixture has thickened.

Remove from the heat and stir in the butter, one piece at a time, until it is all incorporated. Pour the filling into the cooled crust(s). Set aside in a cool place. Allow the curd to solidify.

Make

Make the meringue: In the bowl of a stand mixer fitted with the whisk attachment, whip the egg whites together with the 2 tablespoons sugar and the salt until firm peaks form.

Meanwhile, in a saucepan, melt the remaining 1 cup (200 g) sugar with 3 tablespoons water to make a syrup; heat until the syrup reaches 250°F (121°C) on a candy thermometer, about 10 minutes.

Pour the hot syrup into the egg white mixture while whisking and continue whisking until the meringue is thick and glossy and feels just warm to the touch. Scoop or pipe the foam onto the cooled tart(s).

Quickly brown the top with a crème brulée (kitchen) torch or place the tart(s) under a preheated broiler for a few minutes, turning them to evenly brown the tops. Keep a good eye on the meringue, as it may burn before you know it. Serve.

ETON MESS WITH MINT SUGAR

Serves 6

FOR THE ETON MESS

2¾ ounces (75 g) meringues (see page 212 for pavlova, but I simply use a bag of Christmas meringue cookies from my local bakery)

1 (9-ounce/250-g) bag frozen red fruit

1 cup (250 ml) heavy cream

2 teaspoons confectioners' sugar

FOR THE MINT SUGAR

1 bunch fresh mint

½ cup (100 g) sugar

This is a recipe for the fastest dessert ever—it's pretty much instant. And to make matters worse: It's also terribly delicious.

Prepare

Make the Eton mess: Break the meringues into coarse pieces, cover, and store on the counter. Thaw the red fruit in a bowl in the fridge.

Make

Beat the cream with the confectioners' sugar until fairly thick, not too stiff though; I mean coherent but still soft.

Carefully fold in everything: the pieces of meringue, the thawed fruit, and the whipped cream: It's all right if it looks nicely crude.

For the mint sugar, grind the mint leaves and the sugar into green powder in a food processor. Sprinkle on a plate. Wet the edges of six wide glasses or six nice bowls and dip them in the mint sugar. Carefully spoon the mousse into the glasses, naturally making sure the sugared edges stay undisturbed. Serve right away.

CHOCOLATE-CARAMEL PIE

Serves 10 to 12

FOR THE CRUST

½ cup plus 1 tablespoon (125 g) butter, at room temperature, plus more for the pan

1 cup (125 g) all-purpose flour

¼ cup (30 g) confectioners' sugar

¼ cup (30 g) cornstarch

A pinch of sea salt

FOR THE FILLING

5¼ ounces (150 g) dark chocolate (70% or higher), coarsely chopped

½ cup plus 1 tablespoon (125 g) butter

1 cup (200 g) lightly packed dark brown sugar

⅓ cup (75 ml) heavy cream

1 tablespoon vanilla extract

½ teaspoon sea salt

OPTIONAL

Some cocoa powder for garnish

You can bake this pie completely beforehand. It needs to firm up for 4 hours, which actually makes it perfect for the holidays. This pie is very substantial, so cut small wedges and serve with some crème anglaise (page 255), possibly flavored with some fresh ginger, nutmeg, or espresso.

Prepare

Preheat the oven to 350°F (180°C).

Butter an 8-inch (20-cm) tart pan, preferably one with a removable bottom. Line the bottom with parchment paper, leaving a generous overhang around the edges. Butter the paper as well.

Combine all ingredients for the crust in a food processor and pulse until everything comes together nicely. You can do this by hand, but make sure to work fast. Evenly press out the dough into the prepared tart pan. Use a spatula or wet hands. Sprinkle with the chopped chocolate and refrigerate, allowing it to firm up for at least 30 minutes.

In a saucepan, combine the butter, brown sugar, and cream over low heat until the sugar has dissolved and the butter has melted. Stir in the vanilla and salt.

Remove the tart pan from the fridge and place it on top of a large baking sheet in case the chocolate filling overflows. Pour the warm butter mixture over the chocolate chunks and carefully slide into the oven.

Bake for about 30 minutes, until the caramel around the edges boils intensely, but the center of the pie not just yet.

Let the pie cool to room temperature on a rack. Store in the fridge to let the pie further stiffen for about 4 hours.

Make

Let the pie come to room temperature, sprinkle generously with cocoa powder if you wish, and serve.

SYRUP PUDDING WITH GINGER & ORANGE

Serves 4 to 6

¼ cup (60 ml) golden syrup or apple syrup, plus more for serving

¾ cup (100 g) all-purpose flour

1½ teaspoons baking powder

A pinch of salt

7 tablespoons (100 g) butter, at room temperature

Heaping ¼ cup (60 g) packed light brown sugar

2 eggs, beaten

1 teaspoon vanilla extract

1 teaspoon ground ginger

1 inch (2.5 cm) fresh ginger, peeled and grated

Zest and juice of ½ orange

Heavy cream or crème anglaise (page 255), for serving

ALSO NEEDED

1 (½-L) pudding mold, or a deep ovenproof bowl with a volume of about 2 cups (500 ml) (a Pyrex measuring cup or a Weck mold jar without the lid would be perfect)

Pudding is an Anglo-Saxon term referring to a steamed or cooked cake. You could also call it a poached cake. Syrup pudding is a rather light, sweet cake, a bit sticky as well. I regularly make this cake for winter dinners, with lots of ginger and orange. Nothing beats eating it straight from the bowl while it's still warm and covered in cold unsweetened cream. It's an unbelievably easy-to-make Xmas dessert. If you put it in the oven just before dinnertime you'll have more than enough time to leisurely eat several courses before serving your steaming pudding. It's basically foolproof.

Prepare

Preheat the oven to 400°F (200°C). Place a container (a deep baking pan or other ovenproof container that will comfortably fit your pudding mold later on) on a rack just below the middle position in the oven and fill with hot water until it's two-thirds full. Grease a ½-liter pudding mold with soft butter and pour the syrup into the bottom.

Using a whisk, mix the flour, baking powder, and salt and set aside.

Beat the butter and brown sugar until soft and fluffy. Beat the eggs, vanilla, ground ginger, fresh ginger, and orange zest and juice together, then, while beating, pour into the butter and sugar mixture. Fold in the flour mixture. Pour the batter over the syrup in the mold.

Fold a 1-inch (2.5-cm) pleat into the center of a piece of parchment paper so the pudding has room to expand, then cover the top of the mold with the parchment. Arrange two long sheets of foil in a cross pattern on the countertop, place the mold in the center, and wrap the foil up over the top of the parchment-covered mold and press to thoroughly seal the mold in the foil.

Place the wrapped pudding inside the container of hot water in the oven—the water should come halfway up the side of the mold. Bake for 2 hours, until the cake is nicely risen.

Make

Remove all the foil and parchment and slide a sharp knife between the edge of the mold and the cake, so it will come out easily. The top will be a bit sticky, but that's how it's supposed to be. Invert onto a nice serving plate, decorate with some mistletoe or a twig from the Christmas tree, and serve with some cream or crème anglaise (page 255) and drizzle some extra golden syrup on top. And perhaps something fresh such as home made apple compote.

LEMON SYLLABUB & CRUNCHY OATS

Serves 6

FOR THE COGNAC

7 tablespoons (100 ml) cognac

Grated zest and juice of 2 lemons

A pinch of crushed mace

FOR THE CRUNCHY OATS

Heaping ½ cup (50 g) rolled oats

2 tablespoons confectioners' sugar

1 tablespoon butter

A pinch of freshly grated nutmeg

A pinch of sea salt

A pinch of cinnamon

FOR THE SYLLABUB

1¼ cups (300 ml) heavy cream

5 tablespoons (60 g) sugar

Freshly grated nutmeg

Syllabub is an English dessert that dates back to the sixteenth century. In those days it was made with wine and whipped cream and stored overnight in a cool spot. That way the alcohol curdled the cream, separating the mixture into two layers: delicious cream on top and delicious wine at the bottom. People used long spoons or a special sippy glass to drink the wine through the cream. You could do the same with this dessert: Make the entire dessert and leave it to curdle overnight. I, however, prefer the newfangled way: frothy whipped cream with crumb on the bottom. A ridiculously easy dessert that really can be made in the blink of an eye. You can probably make up your own variations; the possibilities are endless.

Prepare

Combine the cognac, lemon zest and juice, and mace in a bowl, cover, and refrigerate overnight.

Make the crunchy oats: Preheat the oven to 350°F (180°C).

Mix all ingredients for the oats on a parchment paper–lined baking sheet and bake for 8 to 10 minutes, until golden brown and crispy. Turn halfway through the baking time. Set aside until ready to serve.

Make

Beat the cream with the sugar until nearly stiff. Strain the cognac through a sieve into the whipped cream and fold it in. Crumble the crunchy oats and divide among six glasses. Pour the soft whipped cream on top, grate some nutmeg over the desserts, and serve them right away.

Recipes for Christmas

with Compliments from

FIVE STAR

Merry Xmas

Almond Icing

You'll need:

1 lb. ground almonds
10 ozs. castor sugar
10 ozs. icing sugar
3 whole eggs
Few drops almond essence
1 tablespoon sherry

Method:

Mix dry ingredients together. Mix liquid ingredients together. Add enough liquid to dry ingredients to get firm paste. Knead well to make smooth paste.

Royal Icing

You'll need:

1 lb. icing sugar
3–4 egg whites
2 teaspoons lemon juice

Method:

Sieve icing sugar. Put egg whites in a bowl and add icing sugar slowly, beating well either with a wooden spoon or in a mixer. Beat in lemon juice.

For snow scenes, add sugar until mixture stands in points. For piping it should not be quite as stiff.

Cover with a cloth as soon as icing is made, and during use, to keep it from hardening.

FIVE STAR
Rich Christmas Cake

You'll need:

1 lb. Odlum's Cream Flour
1 lb. currants
1 lb. sultanas
1 lb. raisins
8 oz. cherries
8 ozs. chopped almonds
4 ozs. mixed peel
2 ozs. chopped crystallised ginger
1 chopped cooking apple
14 ozs. butter or margarine
14 ozs. brown sugar
4 ozs. ground almonds
1 teaspoon ground nutmeg
1 teaspoon mixed spice
1 teaspoon grated lemon rind
1 glass whiskey or brandy
8 eggs
½ teaspoon salt

Method:

1. First prepare the fruit. Wash the currants by placing them in a strainer and running very hot water through until it runs clear. Then spread currants out onto a teatowel and leave in a warm place to dry. (A hot press is ideal.) Raisins and sultanas need not necessarily be washed, but doing so results in a moister cake. Washing is done in the same way as for currants. Almonds are blanched by pouring boiling water over them and leaving for 15 minutes. Then skins can be easily pinched off. Chop the almonds. The rest of the fruit need not be washed but merely chopped if required. Put all the fruit (except ground almonds and spices) together into a bowl and pour the spirit over them.

2. Next prepare the tin. Use a 12″ round tin or an 11″ square. The tin should be lined with a layer of brown paper and then a double layer of greaseproof paper or a single layer of tinfoil. The lining paper should stand about 2″-3″ above the side of the tin.

3. The mixture is prepared by creaming the butter or margarine with the sugar until light fluffy. Add the eggs (which have been slightly warmed to prevent curdling) one by one to the mixture, beating well. If curdling starts add a little flour in with each egg. (Bad curdling in a cake can be the cause of fruit falling.) Then when all the eggs are added stir in flour which has been sifted with the spices and mixed with the ground almonds. (Avoid beating the flour in as it toughens the mixture.) Stir in the fruit gently, but well, and turn into prepared tin. Make a very slight hollow in the centre.

4. Bake the cake in the centre of the oven which has been pre-heated to "Very Moderate"—"Slow," 325°F, or Gas Mark 3. After the first half hour turn the oven down to 300°F, or Gas Mark 1-2. Leave for a further 3¼ hours. After 1½ hours check cake. If the top looks nicely browned, lay a piece of paper across the top of the cake so it rests on the side lining without touching the cake. This cover will prevent top getting too brown while the centre cooks. Test the cake by sticking a metal skewer or knitting needle into the centre. If it comes out clean with no sticky particles adhering the cake is cooked. Let cake cool in tin. To store: Wrap in greaseproof paper and then put in an airtight tin, or wrap carefully in tinfoil, sealing the seams so that it is airtight.

Recipes from my mother's archive that I kept from Ireland, around 1970

In Paris with Marie, winter 2015

HAZELNUT MERINGUE LOG WITH FRANGELICO CREAM & CARAMEL

Serves 6

FOR THE HAZELNUT MERINGUE

4 egg whites

1 teaspoon cornstarch

1 teaspoon white wine vinegar

A pinch of sea salt

⅔ cup (150 g) firmly packed light brown sugar

Scant 1 cup (125 g) hazelnuts, finely chopped in a food processor

FOR THE FILLING

7 tablespoons (100 ml) heavy cream

8 ounces (250 g) mascarpone

3 to 4 tablespoons Frangelico (hazelnut liqueur)

1 teaspoon vanilla extract

FOR GARNISH

1 bag (about 6 ounces/180 g) soft caramels

2 to 4 tablespoons milk if needed

Confectioners' sugar

This dessert is very quick because the meringue needs only 20 minutes in the oven. You can even bake it the afternoon before your dinner. In that case, leave the meringue rolled up in a dish towel and add the filling right before serving. Don't wait too long, though: The longer it's lying there rolled up, the less frothy the meringue is going to be.

There's no one who doesn't love a thin roll of hazelnut meringue, smeared with a mixture of mascarpone and whipped cream and flavored with Frangelico liqueur and vanilla. (You can use amaretto for an almond flavor instead.) And drizzled with caramel sauce, it's bound to be a beloved staple in your Christmas repertoire.

Prepare

Preheat the oven to 335°F (170°C). Line an 8 by 12-inch (20 by 30-cm) rimmed baking sheet with parchment paper.

In a spotless, dry bowl, whisk the egg whites together with the cornstarch, vinegar, and salt until soft peaks form. Add the brown sugar, a spoonful at a time, making sure to continue whisking until the sugar is incorporated before adding the next spoonful. Whisk until stiff and glossy. Gently fold in ¾ cup plus 2 tablespoons (75 g) of the hazelnuts with a rubber spatula.

Spread out the egg white mixture in the prepared baking sheet. Sprinkle with the remaining hazelnuts. Bake for 20 minutes. The meringue should have a pale, light golden color and feel bouncy to the touch. Let cool for 5 minutes. Invert the meringue onto a clean kitchen towel and peel away the parchment paper. Roll up the meringue from a short side, with the towel standing in as a filling. This way the roll will be pre-formed into the shape it should hold later and it also prevents it from drying out, which may cause the meringue to tear. Store on the counter until ready to fill.

Whip the cream until just about stiff. Beat in the mascarpone and flavor with the liqueur and vanilla. Refrigerate until ready to serve.

Put the caramels in a saucepan on the stove before you join the table, but don't melt them just yet.

CONTINUED

Make

Carefully unroll the meringue. It may tear a little, but that won't matter—this dessert is forgiving.

Spread the cream mixture over the meringue, leaving a margin of ¾ inch (2 cm) on one short end. Very delicately roll up the meringue, starting from the opposite short end, and place the roll on a serving platter.

Melt the caramels in the saucepan over low heat until they form a runny sauce; you can help it along a bit by stirring in a splash of water or milk—often 2 to 4 tablespoons will do the trick. Pour the sauce onto the meringue log in thin trickles. Generously sprinkle with confectioners' sugar. Decorate with some mistletoe to add a special Christmas touch.

WHITE CHOCOLATE–OAK JARS WITH SMOKY TEA SHORTBREAD

Makes about 8 jars

FOR THE WHITE CHOCOLATE–OAK CREAM

1⅔ cups (400 ml) heavy cream

¼ cup (25 g) oak chips or chunks (don't use fine wood shavings!)

8¾ ounces (250 g) white chocolate, in small chunks

FOR THE SMOKY TEA SHORTBREAD

1½ cups (200 g) all-purpose flour

7½ tablespoons (60 g) cornstarch

¼ teaspoon sea salt

1 cup (225 g) butter, at room temperature

½ cup (50 g) sifted confectioners' sugar

Seeds from 1 vanilla bean

1 generous tablespoon lapsang souchong (smoked) tea leaves, very finely ground in a mortar or a food processor

It does sound strange, of course: oak in a dessert. But it really is a delicious flavoring. You let the oak chips steep in the cream, giving it a light smoky, caramel-like flavor. Try for yourself; the sweet white chocolate can perfectly handle some smoke. And if you can't find oak chips, or you feel like trying out something different, you can also use lapsang souchong or Earl Grey tea.

Prepare

Make the white chocolate–oak cream: Put half of the cream and the wood chips in a saucepan over low heat and cook for 30 minutes. Remove from the heat. Strain the cream through a sieve and pour it back into the pan. Add the white chocolate chunks and let them slowly melt in the hot cream.

Allow the white chocolate–oak cream to cool to lukewarm. Stir occasionally.

Whip the remaining cream until stiff. Carefully fold in the white chocolate–oak cream and pour the mixture into pretty (mason) jars or small teacups.

Allow to firm up in the fridge for at least 4 hours. Remove them only when you're about to serve dessert.

Make the smoky tea shortbread: Sift the flour, cornstarch, and salt into a mixing bowl and set aside.

Using a hand mixer, beat the butter together with the confectioners' sugar until fluffy. It will take a good minute or three. Add the vanilla seeds and ground tea. Spoon in the flour mixture and stir until the dough just starts to come together, but no further. Kneading or stirring just briefly is the secret here; you want the cookies to remain crumbly after they've been baked. Roll the dough into a thick sausage and tightly wrap in plastic wrap. Allow the dough to rest in the fridge for at least 1 hour.

Preheat the oven to 350°F (180°C). Line a baking sheet with parchment paper.

Cut the dough sausage into thin slices (say, ⅛ inch/3 mm) and use a metal spatula to place them, evenly spaced, on the lined baking sheet. Bake in the middle of the oven for 12 to 14 minutes, until the edges start to brown. Let cool on the baking sheet for a bit, then transfer them to a rack to cool down further. Repeat until you have used up all the dough.

You can keep these cookies for a couple of weeks in an airtight container or jar. Of course you will serve them with your jars of mousse, and I can assure you there won't be any left to store afterward.

Preserved fruit, Connemara, Clifden, Ireland, 2017

Kept advertisement from my mother's recipe archive from Ireland, around 1970

MINI CHRISTMAS PUDDINGS WITH BRANDY CRÈME FRAÎCHE

Makes 12

½ cup (125 ml) brandy or cognac

Heaping 1 cup (150 g) raisins

Heaping 1 cup (150 g) currants

Heaping ⅓ cup (75 g) succade (preserved or crystalized fruit), chopped

¾ cup (100 g) pitted dates, chopped

3 tablespoons honey or syrup

Grated zest and juice of 1 orange

¾ cup (100 g) all-purpose flour

1 teaspoon speculaas spices

1 teaspoon ground cinnamon

½ teaspoon freshly grated nutmeg

1 tablespoon ground ginger

A pinch of sea salt

1 cup (100 g) dry breadcrumbs

½ cup (100 g) lightly packed brown sugar

⅓ cup (150 g) cold butter, cubed, plus more for the muffin tin

2 eggs, beaten

FOR THE BRANDY CRÈME FRAÎCHE

1¼ cups (300 ml) crème fraîche

3 tablespoons brandy, or more if you wish to flambé

2 tablespoons confectioners' sugar

A real Christmas pudding you need to start in October. And it should be done on "stir-up Sunday": That's the day that everyone starts their pudding. The joke is that the steamed cake should be drizzled with liquor for weeks to come until Christmas. Not only does this preserve it, but the flavor also intensifies enormously.

If you didn't think to make it in advance, or simply don't have time to tend a pudding for two months, you can do it like this. Because you make these mini puddings in muffin tins, they are ready more quickly and you immediately have a lot of them. This is the most delicious dessert ever, and it's ready before you gather at the table. Very relaxed.

Prepare

Pour the brandy over all the dried fruit in a bowl. Mix in the honey and orange zest and juice. Ideally you'd let this stand overnight, but if you don't have a night to spare, let it stand for at least 1 hour.

Preheat the oven to 350°F (180°C). Place a large roasting pan halfway filled with boiling water on a rack just below the middle.

In a bowl, stir the flour with the spices and salt with a whisk, then stir in the breadcrumbs and brown sugar. Rub in the butter with your hands until you get a coarse texture. Scoop in all the soaked fruit and the beaten eggs and stir well.

Butter a 12-cup muffin tin and fill the cups with the batter.

Cover the tin with a sheet of parchment paper and then wrap thoroughly in heavy-duty aluminum foil.

Place the tray in the pan with boiling water in the oven and bake the puddings for 1 hour. Keep them wrapped until ready to serve.

Stir the crème fraîche and then stir in the brandy and confectioners' sugar. Keep covered in the fridge until ready to serve.

Make

Preheat the oven to 350°F (180°C).

Unwrap the puddings and reheat in the oven for 20 minutes. Invert them on the counter and arrange on serving plates. Flambé if you wish (see instructions opposite). Scoop a dollop of crème fraîche alongside each and serve immediately.

Flambé?

Heat a few inches of very strong liquor (like cognac, or something with more than 40% alcohol) in a saucepan. Place the cakes in a safe spot, but so that everyone can see them, and turn off nearly all the lights (you still have to be able to see what you're doing). Hold a lighter above the pan and use a wooden ladle to carefully spoon the burning liquid over the puddings.

CREAM PUFF TREE WITH WHITE CHOCOLATE

Serves 15 (2 cream puffs per person)

Heaping ⅓ cup (50 g) shelled unsalted pistachios

About 13 ounces (370 g) white chocolate

About 30 cream puffs

So, I'm always a big fan of making everything yourself. But with Christmas, anything is allowed. You have such an insane amount to do that I, for the first time in my life, would like to give you a ridiculously easy recipe, an all-store-bought recipe, for which you'll still receive oohs and aahs!

Most supermarkets will sell cream puffs, but if you make a bit of an effort, you could ride your bike to a pâtissier, as chances are their cream puffs are even better.

Buy good chocolate and pretty green pistachios. Let your children or nieces and nephews put it all together and garnish. This way you can cross a dessert for fifteen people off your to-do list at once.

Christmas dessert: Check!

Prepare

Coarsely chop the pistachios.

Break the white chocolate into chunks and melt them *au bain marie* like this: Warm a few inches of water in a saucepan over low heat. Fit a heatproof bowl on top of the pan, and make sure the bottom of the bowl doesn't touch the water. Let the chocolate melt gently in the bowl.

Keep the water at a near boil and stir the chocolate regularly. Remove from the heat once half of the chocolate has melted. The rest will melt automatically. Go slowly: If you stir too fast, there will be condensation in the bowl; if the chocolate becomes too hot and starts to curdle, you will need to start over.

Dip the tops of the cream puffs in the chocolate. Make a circle of puffs on a plate, and stack the puffs in ever smaller circles. If the cream puffs slide away, place the tower in the fridge so the chocolate stiffens faster. Then continue. Work quickly. While the chocolate is still fluid, sprinkle the pistachios on top. Let the tree firm up entirely in the fridge until ready to serve.

Make

Take the cream puff tree out of the fridge, garnish with some Christmas loudness, like stars and decorations from the real tree, and place it on the table. Everyone can tear off the cream puffs themselves.

CHAMPAGNE MOUSSE WITH FIGS IN CHAMPAGNE—BAY LEAF SYRUP

Serves about 6

FOR THE MOUSSE

2 (¼-ounce) envelopes unflavored gelatin powder, or 5 gelatin sheets

2 eggs, separated

1 cup (250 ml) champagne or crémant

¼ cup (50 g) sugar

¾ cup plus 1 tablespoon (200 ml) heavy cream

FOR THE FIGS

2 cup (500 ml) champagne or crémant

1 cup (200 g) sugar or less (to taste)

4 bay leaves

About 12 fresh figs

Prepare

Make the mousse: If using powdered gelatin, sprinkle it over ¼ cup (60 ml) cold water in a cup and let stand until softened, 5 to 10 minutes. (Soak gelatin sheets in a bowl of cold water until softened, then drain and squeeze out the excess water.)

In a heatproof bowl, with a whisk, beat the egg yolks with the champagne and sugar. Place the bowl on top of a pan with 1 inch (2.5 cm) of gently boiling water and continue beating until the sugar has dissolved and the champagne mixture thickens: This takes about 12 minutes. Add the softened gelatin and beat until it has dissolved.

In a squeaky-clean bowl, beat the egg whites into stiff peaks.

Whip the cream until stiff in a third bowl.

First fold the egg whites into the mousse and then the cream. Scoop into a pretty bowl. Place the bowl in the fridge to stiffen for at least 3 hours.

Make the figs: Bring the champagne, sugar, and bay leaves to a gentle boil. Cook for 10 minutes over low heat to reduce to a syrup, then add the figs and let them poach for 10 minutes at a near boil. Pour the syrup with the figs into a large bowl. Let everything cool. You can keep the figs in syrup for a couple of days in the fridge, so just make a lot.

Make

Halve the figs and arrange them over the champagne mousse. Pour some syrup over them and serve the rest of the syrup in a pitcher at the table.

MAKING PEPPERMINT CANDIES

7 tablespoons (100 g) cream cheese,
at room temperature

2 tablespoons butter,
at room temperature

2 or 3 drops peppermint oil

About 2¾ cups (350 g) confectioners'
sugar, plus generous extra

*With an electric mixer, mix all ingredients into an airy batter.
It will first feel a little stiff and dry, but after about 2 minutes it will all
come together. If it's really too dry, add 1 tablespoon milk.*

Shape about 40 small balls of this mixture, each about 1 inch (2 cm).

Space them out over a large sheet of parchment paper.

*Roll each ball through confectioners' sugar and press it flat with
a festive stamp (or with a fork or your thumb).*

Let the peppermints dry before serving.

*Keep them in an airtight container at room temperature
and then in the fridge after a couple of days.*

PANTRY

BASICS

Often in this book, I'll refer to ingredients or additions that are recipes in themselves. And I hear you think: "How do I make that again?" No worries, Van Boven lays it all out for you.

BEEF STOCK

Replace the bones with bones from a deer or wild boar for a venison or pork stock. Or use a mix of bones. Anything is possible.

- 18 ounces (500 g) beef bones (ask your butcher)
- 2 beef shanks (about 18 ounces/500 g)
- 2 onions, not peeled, halved
- 1 small bunch fresh thyme
- A few bay leaves
- A few cloves garlic, not peeled
- 4 to 5 tablespoons olive oil
- 1 bunch celery, cut into thirds
- 2 leeks, rinsed and coarsely chopped
- 1 large carrot, scrubbed and chopped
- 1 bunch fresh parsley
- 3 or 4 pieces of mace
- 1 tablespoon black peppercorns
- 2 tablespoons coriander seeds
- Sea salt and freshly ground black pepper

Preheat the oven to 350°F (180°C).

Put the bones, shanks, onions, thyme, bay leaves, and garlic in a roasting pan. Pour some oil over everything and toss. Roast until the bones are lightly colored. Transfer everything to a large soup pot. Pour in at least 4 quarts (4 L) water and add the remaining ingredients except the salt and ground pepper. Bring to a boil. Lower the heat and let the stock reduce over very low heat for about 3 hours. Occasionally, skim the foam off the stock with a skimmer. If you don't do it, your stock will become cloudy. Sieve the stock or pour it through a colander in which you've placed a clean kitchen towel. Let cool. Put the stock in the fridge. Skim off the congealed fat as soon as the stock is cold. Season the stock with salt and pepper. I often add some Worcestershire sauce and sometimes some salty soy sauce, so the stock develops a richer flavor and color.

CHICKEN STOCK

Replace the chicken (or the chicken carcass) with the carcass from a pheasant or partridge, for a fowl stock.

- 1 whole stewing chicken
- 2 onions, not peeled, halved, with 4 whole cloves stuck in them
- ½ bunch celery, cut into thirds
- 2 leeks, rinsed and coarsely chopped
- 1 large carrot, scrubbed and chopped
- 3 cloves garlic, not peeled
- 3 bay leaves
- 1 small bunch fresh parsley
- 1 small bunch fresh thyme
- 1 tablespoon black peppercorns
- 2 tablespoons coriander seeds
- 3 or 4 pieces of mace
- Sea salt and freshly ground black pepper

Place everything except the sea salt and the ground pepper in a large pot. Pour in 5 to 6 quarts (5 to 6 L) cold water and bring to a boil. Lower the heat. Allow the broth to reduce by half over low heat for 3 hours and carefully skim off the foam from the surface with a skimmer. If you don't do this, your broth will become cloudy. Let the broth simmer for another 3 hours over very low heat, until it's reduced by half. Sieve or pour the broth through a colander in which you've placed a clean kitchen towel. Let cool. Place the broth in the fridge. Once it's cold enough, skim off the congealed fat. Season with salt and pepper.

VEGETABLE BROTH

I'll often add turnips to the broth if they're around. The more vegetables, the better, in fact.

- 2 onions, not peeled, halved, with 4 whole cloves stuck in them
- 1 celeriac, peeled and chopped
- 1 bunch celery, cut in three
- 2 leeks, rinsed and coarsely chopped
- 3 large carrots, scrubbed and chopped

6 cloves garlic, not peeled

3 bay leaves

1 small bunch fresh parsley

1 small bunch fresh rosemary

2 small bunches fresh thyme

1 tablespoon black peppercorns

2 tablespoons coriander seeds

3 or 4 pieces of mace

Sea salt and freshly ground black pepper

Place everything except the salt and ground pepper in a large pot. Pour in 5 to 6 quarts (5 to 6 L) cold water and bring to a boil. Lower the heat and allow the broth to reduce by half, about 2 hours over low heat. Carefully skim off the foam from the surface with a skimmer—otherwise your broth will become cloudy. Sieve the broth or pour through a colander in which you've placed a clean kitchen towel. Let cool. Season the broth with salt and pepper.

CLASSIC VINAIGRETTE

I'll often write below a recipe: "Goes well with a green salad." Here's a simple recipe for the vinaigrette.

1 tablespoon sharp (Dijon) mustard

A pinch of sea salt

Freshly ground black pepper

4 tablespoons (60 ml) white wine vinegar

7 to 8 tablespoons (105 to 120 ml) light olive oil

Put the mustard in a bowl. Add the salt, pepper, and vinegar and stir with a small whisk until the salt has dissolved. While stirring, pour in the oil in a thin trickle. If needed, thin with a drop of cold water.

Variations

For a sweeter vinaigrette, add 1 tablespoon honey or ginger syrup.

Add a diced shallot.

Add very finely chopped capers, fresh tarragon, and red onion (nice with boiled potatoes).

Use other kinds of mustard (for example coarse, violet), other kinds of vinegar (raspberry vinegar, red wine vinegar), or other kinds of oil (hazelnut or walnut for example; in that case, use half nut oil, half regular oil or the flavor becomes too strong).

CRÈME ANGLAISE

This is a recipe for more than a quart, so feel free to make only half if you don't need as much.

1 quart (1 L) milk

2 vanilla beans

12 egg yolks

1¼ cups (250 g) sugar

Put the milk in a saucepan and scrape in the vanilla bean seeds; add the vanilla bean pods as well. Bring to a low simmer and heat for 10 minutes.

Beat the egg yolks with the sugar until foamy and the sugar has dissolved. Scoop the vanilla bean pods out of the milk, and add a portion of the hot vanilla milk to the beaten egg yolks. Stir well and pour everything into the pan. Bring to a gentle boil and stir for about 3 minutes, until the crème thickens.

The crème anglaise is ready when it coats the back of a wooden spoon and you can draw a line in the crème that doesn't close. Let cool and refrigerate with a sheet of plastic wrap directly on top of the crème anglaise so it doesn't form a skin.

CUSTARD

Custard is the thick brother of crème anglaise.

3¾ cups (900 ml) milk

2 vanilla beans

9 egg yolks

1 cup (200 g) sugar

1½ tablespoons all-purpose flour

Put the milk in a saucepan and scrape in the vanilla bean seeds; add the vanilla bean pods as well. Bring to a low simmer and heat for 10 minutes.

Beat the egg yolks with the sugar and flour until foamy and the sugar has dissolved. Scoop the vanilla bean pods out of the milk and pour a portion of the hot vanilla milk in with the beaten eggs. Stir well and pour everything back into the pan. Bring to a gentle boil and stir for about 3 minutes, until the custard has sufficiently thickened.

The custard is ready when it has the consistency of thin yogurt. Let cool and refrigerate with a sheet of plastic wrap directly on top of the custard so it doesn't form a skin.

ONION-GINGER COMPOTE

TART BEETS

HORSERADISH MUSTARD

ONION-GINGER COMPOTE

Makes 1 jar (1¾ cups/450 ml)

2 tablespoons butter

1 pound (500 g) onions, thinly sliced

1 large cooking apple (like Reinette, Elstar, or Golden Delicious), peeled and diced

About 3 inches (8 cm) fresh ginger (a good chunk), peeled and grated

1 tablespoon fresh thyme leaves

1 teaspoon sea salt

7 tablespoons (100 ml) apple cider vinegar

3 to 4 tablespoons honey, or to taste (optional)

Nice with cold meat, like ham or roast beef, or with cheese or pâté, like the wild rabbit terrine on page 109.

In a heavy-bottomed pot, melt the butter and braise the onions, while occasionally stirring, until they are nice and soft, about 15 minutes. Add the apple, ginger, thyme, salt, and vinegar and let everything simmer over very low heat until the compote is light brown and the onions and apple are completely tender.

Add a drop of water if it's too dry.

Season the compote with some honey, but you can go without if you like it as is.

Refrigerate in a sterile jar. It easily keeps for a month or two.

TART BEETS

Makes 2 jars (1¾ cups/ 450 ml each)

8 to 10 medium red beets

1¼ cups (300 ml) white wine vinegar

½ cup plus 2 tablespoons (150 ml) dry white wine

6 tablespoons (75 g) sugar

1 tablespoon coarse salt

1 tablespoon coriander seeds

1 tablespoon mustard seeds

½ tablespoon chile flakes (or to taste)

4 whole cloves

6 bay leaves (preferably fresh)

Go easy on yourself. Serve a charcuterie platter from the finest butcher in your neighborhood as an appetizer (or the terrine on page 109) and serve some preserved beets alongside. That way it's still a bit "home made."

This quantity will last you through all of December.

Cook the beets in a large saucepan of water for about 45 minutes, until tender. Drain and peel. Cut into wedges and place in a large stainless-steel bowl or in glass canning jars.

Heat the vinegar, wine, 1 cup (250 ml) water, the sugar, and salt in a saucepan and add the coriander seeds, mustard seeds, chile flakes, cloves, and bay leaves. Stir until the sugar has dissolved, then pour the mixture over the beets.

Let cool and transfer to sterile jars. Place in the fridge for at least a day, and preferably for about 4 days, to let the flavors develop.

If well covered, you can keep the beets for a month to a month and a half.

HORSERADISH MUSTARD

Makes ½ jar (⅞ cup/200 ml)

5 tablespoons (50 g) mustard seeds, pulverized to powder in a mortar

1 tablespoon finely grated fresh horseradish, or 2 tablespoons from a jar

2 tablespoons olive oil

7 tablespoons (100 ml) apple cider vinegar

1 teaspoon sea salt

1 small clove garlic, crushed in a mortar

Grated zest of ¼ lemon, or to taste

This recipe is after Darina Allen's recipe from *Forgotten Skills of Cooking*.

A delicious sharp and fresh mustard to serve with pâté—for example, the wild rabbit terrine on page 109—or red meat or cold meatballs.

Combine everything and let stand for a day in a clean jar. This way the mustard thickens a little and it can improve in flavor. It tastes even better after a couple of days.

VAN BOVEN'S MINCEMEAT

Makes about 2¼ pounds (1 kg)

¾ cup (100 g) brown raisins

¾ cup (100 g) currants

¾ cup (100 g) sultanas (golden raisins)

¾ cup (100 g) candied fruit or peel, finely chopped

2 tart apples, not peeled, cored, coarsely grated

7 tablespoons (100 g) butter

⅔ cup (150 g) firmly packed dark brown sugar

⅔ cup (75 g) chopped almonds

Grated zest of 1 orange or 2 clementines

½ teaspoon vanilla extract

1 teaspoon ground cinnamon

1 teaspoon ground ginger

½ clove, ground in a mortar

1 teaspoon freshly grated nutmeg

1 teaspoon ground allspice

A pinch of sea salt

⅓ cup (75 ml) white port

⅓ cup (75 ml) brandy, plus extra if needed

Mincemeat. It sounds like ground beef, but that is "minced meat." In Anglican countries, mincemeat equals Christmas, as far as I'm concerned. It is a mixture of finely chopped fruit, spices, dark brown sugar, and liquor that's used primarily as filling for Christmas pies.

But there's so much more you can do with it: Look at my recipe for pheasants filled with mincemeat on page 142, for example.

The first recipes for mincemeat hark back to the fifteenth, sixteenth, and seventeenth centuries, when cooks still worked with kidney fat as a thickening agent for puddings, which weren't always sweet. Often they were hearty, but served with something sweet. Think blood sausage, which also contains many spices, and which we like to eat with baked apple and cinnamon, or think about hearty pancakes with bacon and syrup.

This is how the name for this filling came to be: Because leftover chunks of infrequently used meat, including kidney fat, were used, it received the name mincemeat (ground meat). In Ireland they still use the kidney fat (suet), and it adds another layer to the flavor, similar to how goose fat has that effect on baked potatoes. But I replace it with butter, which tastes just as good and is lots easier for us Dutch.

Because mincemeat requires many ingredients, it's best to make a lot at once. Preserve it in a jar in the pantry, in a cool spot, and you can have fun with it the entire Christmas period.

Put all the dried fruit, the apples, butter, and brown sugar in a saucepan over medium heat. Stir until the butter has melted, then add the almonds, orange zest, vanilla, the spices, and salt.

Let simmer over low heat for 10 minutes. Let cool in a wide bowl. Stir in the liquor, and scoop the mincemeat into squeaky-clean jars.

Let stand for a day or more, to allow the fruits to absorb all the liquid.

You can keep the mincemeat in the fridge, provided you keep it in a clean jar, for 2 to 3 months. If your mincemeat dries out because the dried fruits have absorbed all the liquid, add some more brandy. Alcohol is a preservative, so the mincemeat will keep for a long time.

Paris in the snow

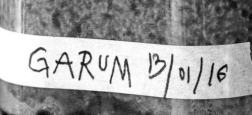

Jars of fermenting fish sauce

FISH SAUCE OR GARUM

Makes scant ½ jar (½ to ⅝ cup/ 150 to 200 ml)

2¼ pounds (1 kg) whole fatty fish, with intestines and everything (for example, sardines, anchovies, mackerel, or herring)

1 cup (130 g) fine kosher salt

This recipe is adapted from one that I once received from the king of the fermenters, Christian Weij. I have many jars full of garum in my pantry. You need some patience to make it, but I've never tasted something so delicious.

This is pure umami: Add a drop of home made fish sauce to any sauce, a bloody mary, or dressing, and your entire dish will transform into something sensational. You'll never want to use ordinary salt in your savory recipes, I promise. Obviously you can buy fish sauce, but it's a different game when it's home made. The Romans did it, so why wouldn't you?

Make sure to really chop the fish very finely, or you'll have to wait years. It goes faster with smaller pieces, and you'll have a bottle of beautiful elixir standing on your counter within the year.

Chop up the fish with skin and bones, gills, heads and all into small pieces, ideally even smaller than a centimeter. It's important to use the whole fish, so brush off your reservations.

Combine the fish with the salt in a large canning jar without the rubber ring (to allow bacteria in the air to contribute to the process) and place the jar somewhere unexposed to direct sunlight.

Shake the jar on occasion when you walk by. Once the fish has turned liquid, and you only see bones floating around, you can start sieving. I place a clean dish cloth in a colander and let the garum slowly seep through. Collect the transparent liquid and pour into a squeaky-clean jar.

Liquid gold.

CRANBERRY COMPOTE

Makes 1 jar (1⅔ cups/400 ml)

½ cup (100 g) lightly packed light brown sugar

Finely grated zest of 1 orange and juice of 2 oranges

9 ounces (250 g) fresh or frozen cranberries

1 tablespoon coarse mustard

2 sprigs fresh rosemary

A pinch of sea salt

Combine everything in a saucepan and bring to a boil. Lower the heat. Let simmer for 8 to 10 minutes, until the berries begin to burst.

Remove from the heat and let cool. Remove the rosemary sprigs before serving, but leave them in long enough for the flavor.

Covered in a clean jar in the fridge, the compote will keep for weeks.

Watercress-Miso Mayo

HOME MADE MAYONNAISE

2 generous cups (500 ml)

Make sure that all ingredients are at room temperature

2 egg yolks

1 teaspoon sharp (Dijon) mustard

Sea salt and freshly ground black pepper

About 1¼ cups (300 ml) sunflower oil

2 tablespoons white wine vinegar

1 to 2 tablespoons fresh lemon juice (to taste)

I advise using this mayo for the Russian potato salad on page 134 and the smoked chicken salad on page 133, but a basic recipe for mayo can always come in handy.

In a bowl, beat the egg yolks together with the mustard, and add some salt and pepper. Add the oil in a thin trickle, while mixing with a hand mixer. Once you've added half of the oil, season the mayonnaise with vinegar and lemon juice. Once the mayonnaise begins to thicken, you can add the oil more quickly.

Season with salt and pepper. Keep cold in the refrigerator until use.

TIP: If the mayo begins to curdle, beat a new egg yolk in a clean bowl and beat in the curdled mayonnaise in a drizzle. Use the rest of the oil in the new mayonnaise.

WATERCRESS—MISO MAYO

2 generous cups (500 ml)

Make sure that all ingredients are at room temperature

1 handful watercress, stems removed, or spinach

2 egg yolks

¼ cup (60 ml) fresh lemon juice

2 teaspoons white miso

Sea salt and freshly ground black pepper

1 tablespoon Dijon mustard

About 1¼ cups (300 ml) sunflower oil

Serve with fish—for example, the salmon on page 141. Or use it for a seafood cocktail. In any case, you'll find a way to use this.

In a blender, process the watercress with the egg yolks, lemon juice, and miso until smooth, adding a tiny bit of salt and pepper if you wish. Miso is also salty, so beware.

Add the oil in a thin trickle, while pulsing the blender at the lowest speed. This way you'll prevent the mayonnaise from curdling. When the mayonnaise begins to thicken, you can add the oil a bit more quickly. Taste whether the flavor is balanced: Sometimes you may want to add some more salt, or only some lemon juice.

Cover the miso mayo and put in the refrigerator until use.

OATCAKES WITH POPPY SEEDS

Makes about 30 cookies

¾ cup plus 2 tablespoons (75 g) old-fashioned rolled oats

1 cup plus 1 tablespoon (100 g) fine oat flour

Sea salt and freshly ground black pepper

About 2 tablespoons poppy seeds

2 tablespoons plus 2 teaspoons olive oil, plus a little extra if needed

7 to 10 tablespoons (100 to 150 ml) boiling water (boil a little more, so you have plenty)

"Rolled oat crackers" sounds so overly healthy, and "oatcakes" sounds much happier, so that's why I used the British name. In Ireland they eat these crunchy toasts with cheese. You can take this recipe in any direction: First toast the oats for a darker effect. Or grind them finely for very delicate crackers. I add poppy seeds, but sesame seeds, very finely chopped olives, or herbs like oregano or rosemary work well too. You'll figure it out. Store them in an airtight container. They'll keep the entire Christmas holiday.

Preheat the oven to 350°F (180°C). Line two baking sheets with parchment paper.

Combine the oats, oat flour, salt and pepper to taste, and poppy seeds in a bowl. Add the oil in a little indentation in the middle, and add as much boiling water as needed to make a dough that is nice and smooth, and not sticky. Work quickly and don't knead too long. The dough should just about come together. Add a little extra oat flour if needed. No stress. This can't fail.

Form into a ball and let rest for 30 minutes. It will absorb all the liquid and become nicely dry. Roll it out on an oatmeal-dusted countertop, and dust with some extra oat flour if it's too sticky. Cut out cookies (each 2½ to 3 inches/6 to 8 cm). Place them on the baking sheets and bake them in batches for 30 minutes, turning the baking sheet halfway through for even browning, until they are crunchy. Let cool on a rack.

MENUS

COLD BUFFET

SERVES 12

You can make this almost entirely in advance

CREAM OF GORGONZOLA &
POACHED PEARS ON TOAST

double the recipe

82

PAPAYA GIN GAZPACHO & OYSTERS

double the recipe

90

TERRINE OF WILD RABBIT & PISTACHIOS

double the recipe
(with everything from pages 258 & 259)

109

MACKEREL TARTLET

make two

128

CELERY ALMOND SALAD

double the recipe

180

VEGETABLE SPIRAL TART
WITH AVOCADO-CURRY CREAM

double the recipe
serve at room temperature

165

PAVLOVA TRIFLE
WITH POACHED PEARS

make two

214

ROMANTIC CHRISTMAS DINNER MENU

SERVES A COUPLE

GIN FIZZ WITH BLACKBERRIES

two glasses each so you're merry; otherwise make half the recipe

61

OYSTERS WITH JALAPEÑO DRESSING

page 69 (check page 90 for how to open oysters)

BEETS, SMOKED CURD & ROASTED BUCKWHEAT

halve the recipe

130

CHARRED OXHEART CABBAGE
WITH TARRAGON, FISH SAUCE & BROWN BUTTER

149

KOHLRABI GRATIN
WITH CARAWAY & FETA

halve the recipe

198

GREEN SALAD
WITH CLASSIC VINAIGRETTE

255

ETON MESS WITH MINT SUGAR

halve the recipe

227

SMALL PLATE MENU

SERVES 8

PAPAYA GIN GAZPACHO & OYSTERS

in small glasses

90

VICTOR'S CRAYFISH COCKTAIL

121

WHOLE SIDE OF SALMON
WITH FENNEL, LEMON &
WATERCRESS–MISO MAYO

141

WARM BEAN SALAD
WITH CASHEW & KALE PESTO

195

CELERY ALMOND SALAD

double the recipe

180

BLOOD ORANGE–MERINGUE TARTLETS

224

FISH & SEAFOOD MENU

SERVES 8

PAPAYA GIN GAZPACHO & OYSTERS
in small glasses
90

POTATO PATTIES WITH CRAB RÉMOULADE
double the recipe
118

RUM-CURED & SMOKED WILD SALMON
151

MUSTARD GRATIN WITH POTATOES & PARSNIPS
187

CELERY ALMOND SALAD
double the recipe
180

LEMON SYLLABUB & CRUNCHY OATS
double the recipe
233

CHRISTMAS BREAKFAST

SERVES 4

BRIOCHE & RED FRUIT SWIRLS WITH RICOTTA GLAZE

23

CHRISTMAS WREATH BREAD

26

CRUNCHY BLACKBERRY & APPLE COCOTTES

42

SAUSAGE BUNS WITH FENNEL

38

Fresh juices

Coffee & tea

Jugs of water with cranberries and a sprig of rosemary

Bread or rolls from the bakery and deluxe charcuterie and cheeses from the butcher and cheesemonger

CLASSIC MINI MINCE PIES

29

CHRISTMAS BRUNCH

SERVES 5

Put everything on the table at once

PUMPKIN, FETA &
SAGE PULL-APART BREAD

35

WILD MUSHROOM SOUP
WITH HAZELNUTS

101

SCOTTISH EGGS

44

PORTOBELLO & PEAR SALAD

115

DUTCH BABY WITH NETTLE CHEESE
& STEAMED LEEKS

170

HAZELNUT MERINGUE LOG
WITH FRANGELICO CREAM & CARAMEL

237

MENU FOR THE VEGETARIAN

SERVES 4

GOUGÈRES AND ROASTED SWEET CHESTNUTS

72 & 74

MUSHROOM TARTLETS WITH GOAT CHEESE & BEETS

112

CELERIAC ROAST WITH CITRUS SAUCE

144

FULL-FLAVORED RED CABBAGE WITH PEARS & HAZELNUTS

192

MASHED POTATOES WITH CELERIAC & APPLE

176

CHOCOLATE-CARAMEL PIE

229

LONG MENU FOR THE VEGETARIAN

SERVES 4

SPICY GOAT CHEESE SPREAD
WITH HOME MADE MELBA TOAST
77

PARSNIP APPLE SOUP WITH CURRY,
CELERY OIL & SMOKED ALMONDS
94

PORTOBELLO & PEAR SALAD
115

ROASTED CAULIFLOWER
WITH GOAT CHEESE CREAM
155

MUSTARD GRATIN
WITH POTATOES & PARSNIPS
187

CARROT TATIN WITH GOAT CHEESE
179

WHITE CHOCOLATE—OAK JARS
WITH SMOKY TEA SHORTBREAD
240

THREE-COURSE MENU

SERVES 6

ROASTED KOHLRABI WITH
CHANTERELLES & RYE BREADCRUMBS

make 1½ recipes

126

MINCEMEAT-STUFFED PHEASANTS
WITH BRANDY SAUCE

142

STUFFED BAKED APPLES

174

MASHED POTATOES WITH CELERIAC & APPLE

176

CHAMPAGNE MOUSSE WITH
FIGS IN CHAMPAGNE—BAY LEAF SYRUP

249

CHRISTMAS DINNER FOR THE ENTIRE FAMILY

SERVES 10 OR MORE

CRANBERRY MARGARITAS

make five recipes' worth in two batches in a large ½-gallon (2-L) canning jar

52

ROASTED SWEET CHESTNUTS

You can leave this to a responsible uncle with the nieces and nephews

74

TERRINE OF TENDER LEEK
WITH SMOKED SALMON & MASCARPONE

double the recipe

111

PUMPKIN CRÈME WITH STAR ANISE & CRAYFISH

triple the recipe

92

CHRISTMAS PORCHETTA

make two

158

MASHED POTATOES WITH CELERIAC & APPLE

make four recipes' worth

176

CARROT TATIN WITH GOAT CHEESE

make four recipes' worth in advance; serve at room temperature

179

TRIFLE WITH SALTY CARAMEL,
CHEESECAKE CREAM & CHEWY BROWNIES

make two

209

FOUR-COURSE MENU

SERVES 6

RABBIT (OR CHICKEN) RILLETTES

123

LEEK & POTATO CRÈME SOUP
WITH FRIED SCALLOPS & PARSLEY OIL

89

GUINEA FOWL WITH
PROSECCO–GREEN GRAPE SAUCE

163

BROCCOLI POT PIES

make six jars (1½ recipes' worth)

185

MUSTARD GRATIN
WITH POTATOES & PARSNIPS

187

LIGHT BROWN PAVLOVA
WITH POACHED PEARS & CHOCOLATE

212

FIVE-COURSE MENU

SERVES 6

MiNi BRiE & WHiSKEY COCOTTES WiTH RAiSiNS & VANiLLA

make 6 (1½ recipes' worth)

117

small plates

CAULiFLOWER CRÈME WiTH COCONUT, CUMiN & PiNE NUTS

102

PASTY OF DEER & ALE

156

FULL-FLAVORED RED CABBAGE WiTH PEARS & HAZELNUTS

192

BRUSSELS SPROUTS À LA CARBONARA

make 1½ recipes' worth

191

CHEESE PLATTER WiTH HOME MADE FRUiT SALAMi

219

COFFEE WiTH MiNCEMEAT FUDGE

223

FOUR-COURSE MENU WITH GAME

SERVES 6

TERRINE OF WILD RABBIT & PISTACHIOS
109

MINCEMEAT-STUFFED PHEASANTS WITH BRANDY SAUCE
make two
142

FULL-FLAVORED RED CABBAGE WITH PEARS & HAZELNUTS
192

BROCCOLI POT PIES
make six jars (1½ recipes' worth)
185

MUSTARD GRATIN WITH POTATOES & PARSNIPS
187

CHEESE PLATTER WITH HOME MADE FRUIT SALAMI
219

HAZELNUT MERINGUE LOG WITH FRANGELICO CREAM & CARAMEL
237

INDEX

INDEX BY COURSE

Mustard gratin with potatoes & parsnips 187

Brussels sprouts à la carbonara 191

Full-flavored red cabbage with pears & hazelnuts 192

Warm bean salad with cashew & kale pesto 195

Oven-roasted beets stuffed with goat cheese, dates & celery 197

Kohlrabi gratin with caraway & feta 198

New potatoes in jackets 201

Apple, walnut, cranberry & brown rice salad 202

Desserts

Trifle with salty caramel, cheesecake cream & chewy brownies 209

Light brown pavlova with poached pears & chocolate 212

Pavlova trifle with poached pears 214

Cheese platter 216–17

Cheese platter with home made fruit salami 219

Warm custard pudding with banana, Belgian waffles & meringue 221

Mincemeat fudge 223

Blood orange-meringue tartlets 224

Eton mess with mint sugar 227

Chocolate-caramel pie 229

Syrup pudding with ginger & orange 230

Lemon syllabub & crunchy oats 233

Hazelnut meringue log with Frangelico cream & caramel 237

White chocolate–oak jars with smoky tea shortbread 240

Mini Christmas puddings with brandy crème fraîche 244

Cream puff tree with white chocolate 246

Champagne mousse with figs in champagne-bay leaf syrup 249

Peppermint candies 251

Pantry

Beef stock 254

Chicken stock 254

Vegetable broth 254

Classic vinaigrette 255

Crème anglaise 255

Custard 255

Onion-ginger compote 258

Tart beets 259

Horseradish mustard 259

Van Boven's mincemeat 261

Fish sauce or garum 265

Cranberry compote 266

Home made mayonnaise 269

Watercress-miso mayo 269

Oatcakes with poppy seeds 270

INDEX BY INGREDIENT & TYPE

Cauliflower crème with coconut, cumin & pine nuts 102

Christmas wreath bread 26

Cream of gorgonzola & stewed pears on toast 82

Pumpkin, feta & sage pull-apart bread 35

Roasted kohlrabi with chanterelles & rye breadcrumbs 126

Sausage buns with fennel 38

Spicy goat cheese spread with home made Melba toast 77

Wentelteefjes, or savory French toast (the Dutch version) 25

Brie

Mini brie & whiskey cocottes with raisins & vanilla 117

Brussels sprouts

Brussels sprouts à la carbonara 191

Buckwheat

Beets, smoked curd & roasted buckwheat 130

Cabbage

Broccoli pot pies 185

Brussels sprouts à la carbonara 191

Cauliflower crème with coconut, cumin & pine nuts 102

Charred oxheart cabbage with tarragon, fish sauce & brown butter 149

Curry cauliflower Christmas pasty with almonds & apricots 167

Full-flavored red cabbage with pears & hazelnuts 192

Roasted cauliflower with goat cheese cream 155

Warm bean salad with cashew & kale pesto 195

Cake

Mini Christmas puddings with brandy crème fraîche 244

Syrup pudding with ginger & orange 230

Trifle with salty caramel, cheesecake cream & chewy brownies 209

Campari

Christmas negroni 58

Cannellini beans

Celery almond salad 180

Carrot

Carrot tatin with goat cheese 179

Shrimp bisque & creamy anchovy rouille 105

Vegetable spiral tart with avocado-curry cream 165

Vegetarian Russian potato salad 134

Cashews

Warm bean salad with cashew & kale pesto 195

Cauliflower

Cauliflower crème with coconut, cumin & pine nuts 102

Curry cauliflower Christmas pasty with almonds & apricots 167

Roasted cauliflower with goat cheese cream 155

Celeriac/celery

Celeriac roast with citrus sauce 144

Celery almond salad 180

Oven-roasted beets stuffed with goat cheese, dates & celery 197

Champagne

Champagne bowl with cranberry, pomegranate & clementine 51

Champagne mousse with figs in champagne-bay leaf syrup 249

Chanterelles

Roasted kohlrabi with chanterelles & rye breadcrumbs 126

Cheese

Brussels sprouts à la carbonara 191

Cheese platter 216–17

Cheese platter with home made fruit salami 219

Curry cauliflower Christmas pasty with almonds & apricots 167

Dutch baby with nettle cheese & steamed leeks 170

Gougères 72

Mackerel tartlet 128

Mustard gratin with potatoes & parsnips 187

New potatoes in jackets 201

Portobello & pear salad 115

Roasted kohlrabi with chanterelles & rye breadcrumbs 126

Smoked chicken salad with grapes & Parmesan-tarragon dressing 133

Warm bean salad with cashew & kale pesto 195

Wentelteefjes, or savory French toast (the Dutch version) 25

Chestnuts

Roasted sweet chestnuts 74

Chicken

Rabbit (or chicken) rillettes 123

Smoked chicken salad with grapes & Parmesan-tarragon dressing 133

Terrine of wild rabbit & pistachios 109

Chicory

Smoked chicken salad with grapes & Parmesan-tarragon dressing 133

Chiles

Jalapeño dressing 69

Chocolate

Chocolate sauce 209

Chocolate-caramel pie 229

Cream puff tree with white chocolate 246

Light brown pavlova with poached pears & chocolate 212

Mincemeat fudge 223

Trifle with salty caramel, cheesecake cream & chewy brownies 209

Warm ginger cocoa with roasted marshmallows 49

White chocolate–oak jars with smoky tea shortbread 240

Clementines

Celeriac roast with citrus sauce 144

Champagne bowl with cranberry, pomegranate & clementine 51

Coconut milk

Cauliflower crème with coconut, cumin & pine nuts 102

Cognac

Lemon syllabub & crunchy oats 233

Compote

Cranberry compote 266

Onion-ginger compote 258

Cookies

Krispy Christmas wreaths 30

White chocolate–oak jars with smoky tea shortbread 240

Crab

Potato patties with crab rémoulade 118

Crackers

Oatcakes with poppy seeds 270

Cranberries/juice

Apple, walnut, cranberry & brown rice salad 202

Apple-cranberry Christmas rolls 37

Champagne bowl with cranberry, pomegranate & clementine 51

Cranberry compote 266

Cranberry margaritas 52

Cranberry pine mocktail 58

Krispy Christmas wreaths 30

Crayfish

Pumpkin crème with star anise & crayfish 92

Victor's crayfish cocktail 121

Cream cheese

Cream of gorgonzola & stewed pears on toast 82

Roasted cauliflower with goat cheese cream 155

Terrine of tender leek with smoked salmon & mascarpone 111

Trifle with salty caramel, cheesecake cream & chewy brownies 209

Cream puffs

Cream puff tree with white chocolate 246

Gougères 72

Crème anglaise 255

Crème fraîche

Mini Christmas puddings with brandy crème fraîche 244

Vegetable spiral tart with avocado-curry cream 165

Croutons

Home made croutons 102

Crustaceans

Potato patties with crab rémoulade 118

Pumpkin crème with star anise & crayfish 92

Shrimp bisque & creamy anchovy rouille 105

Victor's crayfish cocktail 121

Cucumber

Gin fizz with blackberries 61

Papaya gin gazpacho & oysters 90

Portobello & pear salad 115

Currants

Christmas wreath bread 26

Mini Christmas puddings with brandy crème fraîche 244

Van Boven's mincemeat 261

Curry

Curry cauliflower Christmas pasty with almonds & apricots 167

Parsnip apple soup with curry, celery oil & smoked almonds 94

Vegetable spiral tart with avocado-curry cream 165

Custard

Custard 255

Warm custard pudding with banana, Belgian waffles & meringue 221

Dates

Cheese platter with home made fruit salami 219

Mini Christmas puddings with brandy crème fraîche 244

Oven-roasted beets stuffed with goat cheese, dates & celery 197

Dip and spread

Cream of gorgonzola & stewed pears on toast 82

Deep-fried pickles with buttermilk dip 81

Spicy goat cheese spread with home made Melba toast 77

Dressing

Classic vinaigrette 255

Jalapeño dressing 69

Smoked chicken salad with grapes & Parmesan-tarragon dressing 133

Eggplant

Vegetable spiral tart with avocado-curry cream 165

Eggs

Advocaat (Dutch eggnog) 63

Scottish eggs 44

Vegetarian Russian potato salad 134

Fava beans

Broccoli pot pies 185

Warm bean salad with cashew & kale pesto 195

Fennel

Sausage buns with fennel 38

Shrimp bisque & creamy anchovy rouille 105

Smoked chicken salad with grapes & Parmesan-tarragon dressing 133

Victor's crayfish cocktail 121

Whole side of salmon with fennel, lemon & watercress-miso mayo 141

Feta

Kohlrabi gratin with caraway seed & feta 198

Pumpkin, feta & sage pull-apart bread 35

Figs

Champagne mousse with figs in champagne-bay leaf syrup 249

Cheese platter with home made fruit salami 219

Fish sauce or garum

Charred oxheart cabbage with tarragon, fish sauce & brown butter 149

Fish sauce or garum 265

Fowl

See pheasant; chicken; guinea fowl

Fruit, red

Brioche & red fruit swirls with ricotta glaze 23

Eton mess with mint sugar 227

Pavlova trifle with poached pears 214

Fudge

Mincemeat fudge 223

Garum or fish sauce

Charred oxheart cabbage with tarragon, fish sauce & brown butter 149

Fish sauce or garum 265

Gin

Christmas negroni 58

Gin fizz with blackberries 61

Papaya gin gazpacho & oysters 90

Sloe gin 54

Ginger

Onion-ginger compote 258

Syrup pudding with ginger & orange 230

Warm ginger cocoa with roasted marshmallows 49

Ginger ale

Pine & ginger drink 58

Goat cheese

Beet soup with port, goat cheese & seed crunch bar 96

Broccoli pot pies 185

Carrot tatin with goat cheese 179

Mushroom tartlets with goat cheese & beets 112

Oven-roasted beets stuffed with goat cheese, dates & celery 197

Roasted cauliflower with goat cheese cream 155

Spicy goat cheese spread with home made Melba toast 77

Gorgonzola

Cream of gorgonzola & stewed pears on toast 82

Gougères 72

Grapes

Guinea fowl with prosecco-green grape sauce 163

Smoked chicken salad with grapes & Parmesan-tarragon dressing 133

Gratin

Kohlrabi gratin with caraway seed & feta 198

Mustard gratin with potatoes & parsnips 187

Green peas

Broccoli pot pies 185

Vegetarian Russian potato salad 134

Guinea fowl

Guinea fowl with prosecco-green grape sauce 163

Haricots verts

Warm bean salad with cashew & kale pesto 195

Oxheart cabbage

Charred oxheart cabbage with tarragon, fish sauce & brown butter 149

Oysters

Oysters with jalapeño dressing 69

Papaya gin gazpacho & oysters 90

Pancakes

Dutch baby with nettle cheese & steamed leeks 170

Oatmeal pancakes 41

Papaya

Papaya gin gazpacho & oysters 90

Parsnip

Parsnip apple soup with curry, celery oil & smoked almonds 94

Vegetable spiral tart with avocado-curry cream 165

Pasty

Broccoli pot pies 185

Curry cauliflower Christmas pasty with almonds & apricots 167

Pasty of deer & ale 156

Pâté

Terrine of tender leek with smoked salmon & mascarpone 111

Terrine of wild rabbit & pistachios 109

Pear

Cream of gorgonzola & stewed pears on toast 82

Full-flavored red cabbage with pears & hazelnuts 192

Light brown pavlova with poached pears & chocolate 212

Pavlova trifle with poached pears 214

Pork rib roast with prune & pear sauce 147

Portobello & pear salad 115

Peas

Broccoli pot pies 185

Vegetarian Russian potato salad 134

Warm bean salad with cashew & kale pesto 195

Peppermints 251

Pesto

Warm bean salad with cashew & kale pesto 195

Pheasant

Mincemeat-stuffed pheasants with brandy sauce 142

Pickle

Deep-fried pickles with buttermilk dip 81

Vegetarian Russian potato salad 134

Pie, sweet

Blood orange-meringue tartlets 224

Chocolate-caramel pie 229

Classic mini mince pies 29

Light brown pavlova with poached pears & chocolate 212

Pavlova trifle with poached pears 214

Pine nuts

Cauliflower crème with coconut, cumin & pine nuts 102

Oven-roasted beets stuffed with goat cheese, dates & celery 197

Pine syrup

Christmas negroni 58

Cranberry pine mocktail 58

Pine & ginger drink 58

Pine syrup 57

Pistachios

Smoked chicken salad with grapes & Parmesan-tarragon dressing 133

Terrine of wild rabbit & pistachios 109

Pomegranate

Champagne bowl with cranberry, pomegranate & clementine 51

Poppy seeds

Oatcakes with poppy seeds 270

Pork

See also bacon

Pork rib roast with prune & pear sauce 147

Sausage buns with fennel 38

Port

Beet soup with port, goat cheese & seed crunch bar 96

Portobello

Portobello & pear salad 115

Potato

Leek & potato crème soup with fried scallops & parsley oil 89

Mashed potatoes with celeriac & apple 176

Mustard gratin with potato & parsnip 187

New potatoes in jackets 201

Parsnip apple soup with curry, celery oil & smoked almonds 94

Potato patties with crab rémoulade 118

Vegetarian Russian potato salad 134

Puff pastry

Broccoli pot pies 185

Carrot tatin with goat cheese 179

Mushroom tartlets with goat cheese & beets 112

Pasty of deer & ale 156

Sausage buns with fennel 38

Pumpkin

Pumpkin crème with star anise & crayfish 92

Pumpkin, feta & sage pull-apart bread 35

Rabbit

Rabbit (or chicken) rillettes 123

Terrine of wild rabbit & pistachios 109

Raisins

Celery almond salad 180

Mini brie & whiskey cocottes with raisins & vanilla 117

Van Boven's mincemeat 261

Rum

Rum-cured & smoked wild salmon 151

Salad

Celery almond salad 180

Crab salad 118

Portobello & pear salad 115

Potato patties with crab rémoulade 118

Smoked chicken salad with grapes & Parmesan-tarragon dressing 133

Vegetarian Russian potato salad 134

Warm bean salad with cashew & kale pesto 195

Salmon

Rum-cured & smoked wild salmon 151

Terrine of tender leek with smoked salmon & mascarpone 111

Whole side of salmon with fennel, lemon & watercress-miso mayo 141

Sauce

Chocolate sauce 209

Citrus sauce 144

Cocktail sauce 121

Creamy anchovy rouille 105

Crème anglaise 255

Fish sauce or garum 265

Home made mayonnaise 269

Horseradish mustard 259

Kale pesto 195

Prosecco grape sauce 163

Prune pear sauce 147

Salty caramel sauce 209

Watercress-miso mayo 141, 269

Sausage

Sausage buns with fennel 38

Scottish eggs 44

Scallops

Leek & potato crème soup with fried scallops & parsley oil 89

Seeds

Beet soup with port, goat cheese & seed crunch bar 96

Oatcakes with poppy seeds 270

Shellfish

Leek & potato crème soup with fried scallops & parsley oil 89

Oysters with jalapeño dressing 69

Papaya gin gazpacho & oysters 90

Shrimp

Pumpkin crème with star anise & crayfish 92

Shrimp bisque & creamy anchovy rouille 105

Sloe berries

Sloe gin 54

Snow peas

Warm bean salad with cashew & kale pesto 195

Soup

Beet soup with port, goat cheese & seed crunch bar 96

Cauliflower crème with coconut, cumin & pine nuts 102

Leek & potato crème soup with fried scallops & parsley oil 89

Papaya gin gazpacho & oysters 90

Parsnip apple soup with curry, celery oil & smoked almonds 94

Pumpkin crème with star anise & crayfish 92

Shrimp bisque & creamy anchovy rouille 105

Wild mushroom soup with hazelnuts 101

Spinach

Mushroom tartlets with goat cheese & beets 112

Spinach-miso mayo 141, 269

Spread

See dip and spread

String beans

Warm bean salad with cashew & kale pesto 195

Succade

Christmas wreath bread 26

Mini Christmas puddings with brandy crème fraîche 244

Van Boven's mincemeat 261

Sugarsnaps

Warm bean salad with cashew & kale pesto 195

Sweet potato

Vegetable spiral tart with avocado-curry cream 165

Tarragon

Charred oxheart cabbage with
   tarragon, fish sauce & brown butter
   149

Smoked chicken salad with grapes &
   Parmesan-tarragon dressing 133

Tart, savory

Carrot tatin with goat cheese 179

Curry cauliflower Christmas pasty
   with almonds & apricots 167

Mackerel tartlet 128

Mushroom tartlets with goat cheese
   & beets 112

Pasty of deer & ale 156

Vegetable spiral tart with avocado-
   curry cream 165

Tea

White chocolate–oak jars with
   smoky tea shortbread 240

Tequila

Cranberry margaritas 52

Terrine

Terrine of tender leek with smoked
   salmon & mascarpone 111

Terrine of wild rabbit & pistachios
   109

Toast

Cream of gorgonzola & stewed pears
   on toast 82

Oatcakes with poppy seeds 270

Spicy goat cheese spread with home
   made Melba toast 77

Trifle

Pavlova trifle with poached pears 214

Trifle with salty caramel, cheesecake
   cream & chewy brownies 209

Venison

Pasty of deer & ale 156

Vermouth

Christmas negroni 58

Vinaigrette, classic 255

Waffles

Warm custard pudding with banana,
   Belgian waffles & meringue 221

Walnuts

Apple, walnut, cranberry & brown
   rice salad 202

Stuffed baked apples 174

Watercress

Crab salad 118

Watercress-miso mayo 141, 269

Whiskey

Mini brie & whiskey cocottes with
   raisins & vanilla 117

Yogurt

Beets, smoked curd & roasted
   buckwheat 130

THANK YOU & MERRY XMAS

Oof
Love, brilliant photographer, cheers to many more Christmases together.

My parents, sister, and sweet family: Mariëtte, Victor, Sophie, Peter, Joris, Laura, Emilie, Maarten, Jaap
Here's to many more Christmas dinners!
Many more! And also to you up there: Cheers, Dad and Jaap.

All my Christmassy friends and my festive in-laws

Joosje Noordhoek
Wonderful to have such a resource for all my questions.
Thank you for all your spirited help and your lovely humor.

Charlot van Scheijden
For your cheerful encouragements, for your endless patience.

Roosje Klap
Queen of fonts, X!

All the special people working at Fontaine Publishers, the Netherlands, and Abrams, New York
What a lovely group of people you are, really.

The sweetest crew from our television show *Koken met Van Boven*
—a whole extra family, just like that.

The editorial staff at *Libelle*, *Volkskrant Magazine*, and *Delicious*
Without you I never would've written so many Christmas recipes,
never could've thought they would one day become the basis of this book.

Henneman Agency: Vanessa, Florentine & Jessie
Thanks to you I could often just concentrate on my own work,
and that *really* is fine sometimes.

All the sweet and extraordinary people at Humanoid: Sandra, Marjolein, Jolien and all the others
The trips to Arnhem have become my favorite ones.
Thank you for helping me pick out such great dresses.

All my neighbors and friends
For your help with eating all the test recipes. Thank you, neighbor Sjeng,
for lending me your Christmas records, getting me into the right mood.

Last but not least: thank you, Marie, my dear little Xmas elf

With my sister underneath the tree, Ireland, mid-'70s